LIFE AND SAYINGS OF ELDER METTAOUS

LIFE AND SAYINGS OF
ELDER METTAOUS

by

Fr Ignatius el Souriany

ST SHENOUDA'S MONASTERY
SYDNEY, AUSTRALIA
2015

LIFE AND SAYINGS OF ELDER METTAOUS

ST SHENOUDA MONASTERY
8419 Putty Rd,
Putty, NSW, 2330
Sydney, Australia

www.stshenoudamonastery.org.au

ISBN 13: 978-0-9941910-7-6

Translated by:
Michael Kozman

CONTENTS

Introduction

The late monk, the Very Rev. Father Mettaous El Suriany, was a great pillar in monasticism, whether at El Surian Monastery or across the monastic life in general. He came to the monastery at a young age of 22 and lived in the monastery for 60 years continuously, in great asceticism and a spirit of worship.

He lived in a humble cell in the monastery, when the opportunity arose in the early 1960's, and he built his cell close to the eastern wall of the monastery's garden and continued to live there as an ascetic until his departure. The Very Rev Father Mettaous read the books of monasticism such as The Paradise of the Desert Fathers, St John Climacus, the Spiritual Elder (Ephram the Syrian), and the sayings of St Isaac the Syrian, and many others. He lived and struggled to attain the same level of monasticism as was taught from those great pillars of monasticism. He did not stop at the outer appearance of asceticism and devotion. His spiritual exercises were very moderate, as he always said: "The middle pathway has delivered many people without many struggles."

It deeply moved us when we lost him and we felt a void in the monastery. He was our spiritual father and the confession father of about half the monks in the monastery. His words gave great comfort to the listener, as they were filled with spiritual wisdom. He won everybody's love by loving them first and so he was respected by everybody. He lived in the desert during his monastic life and was the disciple of the elderly fathers. All his advice to other monks came from the books of the early desert fathers and their life experiences.

The Very Rev Father Mettaous was a source of comfort to any monk for whatever reason. If a monk were in pain and distress from the temptations of the devil, he could visit Father Mettaous and come out comforted and joyous from the words of grace that overflowed his blessed lips and from the peace that filled his heart and mind. He had an angelic countenance that was filled with peace.

The words "Thank The Lord" never departed from his mouth. Even during his sickness, poor health and heavy burdens he was always thankful to God. His countenance was like the countenance of an angel, gleaming and radiating peace and acceptance of his pains and illnesses. His countenance was especially true in the final period of his life, when God tested him with various illnesses. He lost his sight and good health, but God gave him spiritual insight and heavenly wisdom. Father Mettaous is similar to Saint Didymus, who also lost his sight, but God granted him an inner spiritual insight, and he became a great teacher and dean of the School of Alexandria in tough times.

We can truly call Father Mettaous a role model for monks and a life in the desert. He was a spiritual man, who made moderate decisions, had spiritual insight, endured endlessly and thanked God on every occasion, in every condition and for all things.

He was a great role model, who taught us many things. We ask for his prayers on our behalf and the Monastery of El Surian to remember us in front of the Throne of Grace, till we meet again in heaven.

We offer you, our dear reader, this book concerning the story and sayings of this righteous saint, praying that it will be a source of blessing to everyone who reads it. We thank everyone who contributed to the editing and printing of this book.

Through the pleadings of our Lady Saint Mary and the prayers of our beloved pope Abba Shenouda III, may the Grace of God encompass us all. Amen

Bishop Mettaous

Abbot of the Monastery of El Surian

Preface

I thank the Lord from the depth of my heart for allowing me the opportunity and great blessing to live, encounter and personally learn from our beloved monk, The Very Rev Father Mettaous El Suriany. I witnessed most of the stories and events, as I was his disciple. I had a close acquitance with him and I accompanied him in his final stage of illness. What I witnessed was both incomprehensible and marvellous in mysterious ways.

Despite the fact that Fr Mettaous received blessing from serving the late Fr Youssef El Suriany, it cannot measure up to how much he was served by all the other monks when he was personally ill, and bed ridden.

I beg for your forgiveness as I did not write this book, but recorded some of what I knew about his life; whether it was mentioned by his pure mouth, or from what other fathers said about him, or from his beloved who knew him and encountered him personally.

It is truly arduous, even unfair, to summarise and briefly mention this blessed and sweet story of Father Mettaous in only a few lines or pages. His life extended for more than 80 years, of which he spent about 60 years in the monastery. However, we are here to try and shine light on some aspects of his life that are filled with pains and glorification, so that it may support us in our journey on this earth as sojourners, until we meet in the glory of heaven.

This story between your hands, my beloved reader, is the product of a life filled with spiritual experiences. Father Mettaous lived, struggled, fought, experienced and endured many and various temptations. Whenever he talked about monasticism, he would speak in truth and utter experienced advice.

He lived by word and action, practicing what he preached. He assisted, encouraged and guided everyone. He was able to fit this description in the Book of Job: "Surely you have instructed many, and you have strengthened weak hands. Your words have upheld him who was stumbling, And you have strengthened the feeble knees" (Job 4: 3-4)

I thank the Lord for guiding me to produce the life story of this blessed man, and I thank everyone who assisted in the production of the book. I also thank my Father Bishop Mettaous for his love, encouragement and revision of this book.

The Lord can make this blessed life story a source of blessing to whoever reads it and to encourage us all to struggle and be worthy of the eternal inheritance with the Saints. Through the pleadings of our Lady Saint Mary and the great Saint John Kama the Saint of the Monastery, and through the prayers of His Holiness Pope Shenouda III and his partner, Bishop Mettaous, the Abbot of the Monastery. To Him be the glory and honour forevermore. Amen

Father Ignatius El Souriany

Section 1

Chapter One

His Birth and Upbringing

His Birth

"But You are He who took Me out of the womb; You made Me trust while on My mother's breasts. I was cast upon You from birth. From My mother's womb, You have been My God." (Psalm 22: 9-10).

Shawky (Father Mettaous El Suriany) was born on Sunday 23rd of October 1927, the 12th day of Baba, which is the martyrdom of St Matthew the Evangelist. He was born to a righteous father called Hanna Abd El Malek Attalla, who was a deacon to the late Metropolitan Lucas of the region of Kenna. He was unique with his strong and melodious voice. His mother was also a righteous woman called Baheia Soliman from the district of Tramesa of the region of Kenna.

While his mother was pregnant, his father was placed to work in El Dorr, which follows the region of Aswan at the borders of Egypt and Sudan. It was here that Shawky was born. God had already blessed his parents with a beautiful daughter a year and a half before his birth.   She was his only sister. His birth was a joyous occasion to his parents and family.

His Early Childhood

"It is good for a man to bear the yoke in his youth. Let him sit alone and keep silent, because God has laid it on him." (Lamentations 3: 27-28)

When Shawky was six years old, tragedy struck his family. His father died, leaving behind his widowed wife in the prime of her life, with two orphans at a very innocent age. His mother was a religious woman, who loved God with all her heart. She accepted this trial from God with thanksgiving and acceptance, she consecrated her life to serving and bringing up her children close to God. She refused the idea of marrying again, and did not give in to others' advice of getting married to help her raise her children.

She took it upon herself to raise her children in the fear of God from a very young age. Whenever Fr Mettaous would remember his late mother, he would say in his strong Upper Egypt accent: "May God rest her soul in peace; she brought us up and raised us in virtue and righteousness from our childhood." Thus the saying of St Paul is applicable for Fr Mettaous, as it says: " when I call to remembrance the genuine faith that is in you, which dwelt first in your grandmother Lois and your mother Eunice, and I am persuaded is in you also." (2 Timothy 1:5)

When Fr Mettaous's mother wanted to enrol her children in school, she had to move with both of them from the village of El Taramsa to Kenna. Thus, Shawky continued his primary school, followed by high school and finished his studies there.

He graduated with a Bachelor of Engineering after five years of study. At this stage, Fr Mettaous tells us a story that showed how much his mother cared to raise him up in good behaviour. He says: "One time I got in a car for a long trip, and all the passengers were smoking until my clothes smelt of smoke. When I got home, my mother's face changed suddenly, and she started screaming at me, saying "What is this smell? Smoke? Are you smoking? My son, whom I brought up in the fear of God! Why would you smoke and join the people of this world?!" It took me while to calm her down and to explain to her the incident of the car with the smokers. After I had finished, she calmed down and was assured."

His First Longing for Monasticism

"Before I formed you in the womb I knew you; before you were born I sanctified you" (Jeremiah 1:5)

From a young age, Shawky loved the life of solitude and quietness. He used to stay for a long time by himself, praying and reading his Bible. He often went on the roof of his building, where there was a cage of pigeons. He used to sit there and contemplate the stillness and meekness of the pigeons. He did not like to go to weddings and parties, even those of relatives.

Father Mettaous told us that when he was young he always used to tell his parents that he wanted to go to the monastery and become a monk. They would tell him "There is no monastery here!" so he would answer and say, "But I want to be a monk." They would ask him "So how will you go to the monastery?" and he would innocently answer and say "I would get on a donkey and start walking in the desert till I reach the monastery!" His mother used to take these words to heart and would cry, and sometimes would say that these were merely childish dreams.

On this note, he recounts that when his mother – may God rest her soul – found out about his monasticism she said: "I always prayed for him to be a pure man, but not to of leaving me and becoming a monk!"

The christian discipline, with which he was brought up, formed his character. He was a quiet and peaceful man and his love for God was eminent from his prayers and contemplations and simple attitude to monasticism. All of these factors greatly moved him to become a monk. He started thinking of monasticism and life in a monastery...How? Where? And when? He didn't know.

At his time, Sunday School service was new and many servants came from far places to serve and to be a part of it. Shawky being very energetic and youthful, joined the service. He used to love serving with a great attitude and energy, and used to serve in isolated districts and regions.

He recounted a story once that when he finished his service in the district of Keft it was too late in the night to find any transport to Kenna. He then walked from Keft to Kenna on foot! To put this in context, he walked 19 kilometres on foot when he was 17 years old at that time.

He kept all the books of lesson preparations, even after his arrival to the monastery. This showed how valuable the time of service was in his eyes.

Through his service in Sunday School, he came to know Mr Alfy Nashed, who was a very active servant and the founder of 'Saint Mark Group' in Luxor. They formed a very close friendship which he never forgot until his departure. Due to his confidence in his character and spirituality, Shawky shared with Alfy his desire to join a monastery to live the life of monasticism. Alfy advised him first to get employed in a job and then test to see if this desire is from God or not. If it were from God, then the desire would be confirmed and strengthened, and if it was not, then the desire would fade away by itself.

Shawky listened to Alfy's advice, and he left his widowed mother and sister alone and travelled to Cairo to find a job at one of the companies that would suit his qualification, study and experience. From there he was directed to Kafr El Dawwar, where he was employed in a company that manufactures fabric. He spent about a year and a half there and he did not allow his work to interfere with his spiritual life. At the same time, he was serving in the Church of Saint George in Kafr El Dawwar.

Father Mettaous tells us this story

"I used to go out at night to walk, and I would think about monasticism because the desire to become a monk was getting stronger! I used to pray and plead to God with tears and tell Him:

"O Lord, prepare a way for me, what should I do? I long to live with you the rest of my days, but what can I do with my family, who awaits my return? My mother is a widow and my sister an orphan, and they have nobody to take care of them but myself. O Lord, you are the director of everyone, so please direct this matter with Your Righteous Will."

"The calling of monasticism used to occupy my heart like fire and I could not find a way to quiet down these thoughts, but to conform to them and based on this decision, I started planning to go to the monastery." These thoughts reminds us of the saying of one of the Desert Fathers "The love of Christ made me a foreigner to all earthly matters" (Saint Barsunophius)

Chapter 2

A Diligent Monk

The beginning of the journey to the desert:

"I remember you, the kindness of your youth, the love of your betrothal, when you went after Me in the wilderness, in a land not sown." (Jeremiah 2:2) Despite all these mixed emotions and the longing towards the life of monasticism in the monastery, Shawky had not yet visited a monastery in his life! Furthermore, he had no relationship with any monk from any monastery.

The only source of information he had was an old school friend who went before him and became a monk in the monastery of Saint Paula, the first of the hermits, in the eastern desert. The monk's name was Father Tawadros El Anba Paula. They exchanged infrequent mail from time to time.

Shawky sent him a letter informing him of his decision to join the same monastery, so Father Tawadros replied in a letter notifying him of the approval of the monastery fathers to his coming, and he sent him the address of the monastery.

At this point, Shawky had made up his mind to resign from his job and to go directly to the monastery of Saint Paula to join as a monk. He wrote a letter to his family letting them know that he joined the monastery, but he did not include the name of the monastery so that they might not be able to visit him and try and obstruct the way he chose.

He left this letter with one of his colleagues at work, and he told him to mail the letter after he joined the monastery. He prepared a small bag containing some of his personal belongings and essentials, as well as important documents. He set out on his journey by night, so none of his roommates would notice his disappearance. He went straight to a train station to catch a train that would take him to Cairo and from there to the monastery of Saint Paul.

When he reached the train station, Shawky realised he had forgotten his wallet at his residency! So he quickly turned around and went to his residence to get his wallet and then returned to the train station to catch the train going to Cairo.

When he reached Cairo, he saw a bus heading towards Suez (El Seweis) and he remembered that the letters he used to receive from Fr Tawadrous were addressed from "Suez – Zaafarana." So he got on the bus and when he was seated, he asked one of the passengers if the bus went to Zaafarana. The passenger told him that Zaafarana is very far away from Suez, so he quickly got off that bus. He said to himself that, since he did not know anybody in that place, the best place to go to is Saint Mark's Cathedral in Ezbaweya and from there he would ask about how to get to Saint Paul's Monastery.

Shawky then went to Saint Mark's Cathedral in Claude Bek and went inside the small church named after Saint Steven and found a priest. He sat down next to him and asked him the way to Saint Paul's Monastery.

This priest responded by asking why he wanted to know about the monastery of Saint Paul, so Shawky replied saying that he wanted to become a monk there. The priest continued on asking him some personal questions, such as if he were an only child, or if his mother was widowed, or if he had a younger sister he would be leaving behind alone! The priest rebuked Shawky when he found out that his mother was widowed, and he only had a younger sister, saying: "So you're alone, and you want to become a monk? You are a criminal!"

Fr Mettaous comments on this story saying: "I took the priest's blessing and went my way as if I had heard nothing from him. I was certain that my monastic calling was real and valid."

He also recounts that after this last incident, his thoughts were shaken now and then because of what this priest had said to him. He recounted this incident to the late Bishop Theophilus, the Abbot of El Surian Monastery, who calmed him down and comforted him and prayed an absolution for him, until he was calm and regained his confidence.

He wanted to be without blame and harmless, remembering the saying of Saint Paul: "So that He may establish your hearts blameless in holiness before our God and Father at the coming of our Lord Jesus Christ with all His saints." (1 Thess 3:13)

His Arrival at El Surian Monastery instead of Saint Paula's Monastery:

"And has determined their pre appointed times and the boundaries of their dwellings" (Acts 17: 26)

When the young man, Shawky left the church after his meeting with that priest, he stopped thinking about what he should do. Where should he go? How would he behave? He found a deacon teaching hymns to young children, so he approached him and asked him how to get to the monastery of Saint Paula. The deacon then asked one of the young children to escort him to the residency of the monastery of Saint Paula, near the Ezbaweya.

However, it seems to be a Godly intervention that the child did not hear anything except the word "Ezbaweya", and so, out of his good innate nature, he took Shawky to the Ezbaweya, which is the dwelling of El Surian Monastery.

My dear reader, in case you do not know, the Ezbaweya (the dwelling of the Monastery of Saint Mary – El Surian) lies in front of the dwelling of the Monastery of Saint Paula in Atfa el Ganina in the wide valley on Claude Bek Street near the old Patriarchal.

It is true what is said in the bible: "For My thoughts are not your thoughts, Nor are your ways My ways," says the LORD. "For as the heavens are higher than the earth, So are My ways higher than your ways, And My thoughts than your thoughts." (Isaiah 55: 8-9)

We leave the recount of the story to our beloved saint to tell, because the events of that night had a major influence on the history of the El Surian Monastery from that point onwards.
He says:

"I entered the Ezbaweya, not knowing that it is the dwelling of El Surian Monastery, and not the dwelling of Saint Paula's Monastery, which I had intended on going to. I met with one of the elders of the monastery named Theophilus, who turned out to be the Abbot of the Monastery. I greeted him, sat down with him, and told him about my desire and determination to become a monk. He told me about the hardships that would face me if I chose this path, and the wars from temptations, hunger and need. I was determined in my heart to live this life with all its consequences. I showed Bishop Theophilus the power and depth of my request, and I asked him to pray for me and to accept me in his monastery to be one of his children.

I was certain that the grace of God will accompany me and support me all the way in monasticism.

After Bishop Theophilus examined the truth of my words, and my true desire to live the struggle of monasticism, he asked an accompanying father – who was at that time the late Fr Arsanius the Elder – to write for me a letter of recommendation to go with to the monastery, so that he can submit it to the Abbot of the Monastery to be accepted as a monk. The late Bishop Theophilus prayed for me saying: "May the Lord bring forth fruit from you, my son."

Fr Arsanius also advised me of some of the things I needed to know to become a monk and to begin a new life inside the walls of the monastery."

My Dear Reader:

All these events happened while the young man Shawky believed that he was going to Saint Paula's Monastery. It happened that night, as a monk was preparing dinner; he asked him: "Is this not the residency of Saint Paula monastery?" The monk scoffed at him saying: "What monastery, my friend? You are in the Ezbaweya, the dwelling of El Surian Monastery."

" I was not shaken by finding out what had happened, neither was I worried about becoming a monk in El Surian Monastery, even though I knew nothing except its name and its Abbot!"

I said "Lord, I am in Your hands, whichever way You lead me, I will follow, and whichever place You want me to be, there I will go with You." I spent the rest of my night praying fervently so that God may direct me and support me throughout this new path and monastery."

This is the extent to which Shawky, who left the world and came out to ask the Lord's acceptance and love, trusted his life in God's hands. We see him praising with David the Psalmist saying: "My heart said to You, "Your face, LORD, I will seek." (Psalm 27: 8) We also see him being carried with the Apostle Paul in chains on the ship, saying: "We let her drive" (Acts 27: 15)

Going into the Wilderness and arriving at the Monastery:

"So I said, "Oh, that I had wings like a dove! I would fly away and be at rest. Indeed, I would wander far off, and remain in the wilderness" (Psalm 55: 6-7)

On the morning of Thursday 12/05/1949, Shawky Hanna Allah got on the bus heading towards the Alexandrian road. He got off at the rest house region, and from there he went to El Hokaria (Wady El Natroun presently).

The roads leading to monasteries used to be rough and uneven. Thus, in order to reach your destination you needed a guide to lead the way to ensure that you would not get lost in the vast desert. There was a tour guide living in El Koharia, whose name was Hassan El Gezeery. The late Pope Youannes the Nineteenth (the 113th pope) used to love him a lot for his kind heart and good behaviour, to the extent that he gave him the title Hassan Bek El Gezeery.

This tour guide guided Shawky from El Hokaria to El Surian Monastery on foot, a distance of approximately 12 Kilometres. During their walk, Shawky started up a conversation with Hassan about monasticism,; what they do, eat, and how they live. They continued to talk until the walls of the monastery were visible from far. When they reached the door, they knocked on it, and the keeper of the door opened for them and asked them what they wanted. They were welcomed inside very lovingly, which stirred Shawky's emotions deeply.

It was a common thing amongst monks that anybody who comes walking from the rest house to the monastery would have their feet washed by the monks. This ritual was seen as a sign of welcoming them and as a sign of their love to them, as well as to relieve them of the pain of the walk through the desert.

The First Surprise:

"How lovely is Your tabernacle, O LORD of hosts! My soul longs, yes, even faints For the courts of the LORD; My heart and my flesh cry out for the living God." (Psalm 84: 1-2)

As we mentioned previously, Shawky had never visited a monastery in his whole life until this point and therefore he imagined that all the monks' cells were distant from one another. His imagination drew from stories and his honest love for solitude, and he was struck with surprise when he found that all the cells are lined up door to door!

He then heard the voice of The Very Rev Father Sidarous the Great, the Abbot of the Monastery at that time, who greeted him warmly and received his letter of recommendation. The Very Rev Fr Sidarous took Shawky to his new cell on the eastern side of the monastery, where the old cells used to be. It is also important to mention that Very Rev Fr Sidarous the Great was the first father of confession to Fr Mettaous in his long monastic life, which was close to sixty years.

The Period of Testing:

"He was well-reported of by the brothers." Acts 16:2

From the first moment, Brother Shawky Hanna Allah was tested in order to accept him as a monk in the monastery. He fixed his eyes upon the saying of the great father of monks, St Anthony, "Let everybody bless you". He was an example of a monk under testing, keeping all the laws of the monastery and his new life.

In addition to his main work at the monastery, which was

the meeting room of the monastery, he took upon himself the responsibility of taking care of the monks of the monastery in love and great humility.

Most of the monks at the monastery were of old age. Their lives were mostly spent in the monastery, among whom we will mention a few: Very Rev Father Tawadros the Elder, Very Rev Father Daniel the Elder, Very Rev Father Sidarous the Elder, Very Rev Father Mousa the Elder, Very Rev Father Abdel-Malak, Very Rev Father Touma the Elder...etc.

He used to organise and clean their cells, and fill their stone water pots with fresh water, as well as tending to any need they asked of him. He did all of this in great love, humility and sacrifice without complaining or weariness.

Fr Mettaous recounts that he took the blessing of serving the late Father Yacoub the Blind, by tending to his needs and taking care of his cell for him. He recounts how Fr Yacoub taught him the long hymn "Apekran" (which is said in the feast of any saint). For a long time, Fr Mettaous was the only person who knew this hymn, to the extent that Bishop Theophilus used to ask Fr Mettaous to sing that hymn on the feast of saints!

Shawky continued to uphold great love and humility with great enthusiasm until he gained the acceptance of all the fathers of the monastery – without exception. He also gained their approval for monastic ordination in the Monastery of El Surian. From this point onward, the pathway for his monasticism was laid down.

His Blessed Monasticism:

There is no one under heaven like the Christians if they fulfill their calling as there is no higher rank like monks if they keep their rituals. (Paradise of the Monks)

Four months after entering the monastery, everyone agreed that Brother Shawky deserved to be ordained a monk. They wrote a letter of recommendation, and everybody signed it. The abbot of the monastery, Fr Sidarous the Elder, took the recommendation and travelled to Egypt to hand it to Bishop Theophilus, the Bishop of the Monastery. He asked if he would fulfil the desire of the community of the monks to ordain Shawky as a monk. The Bishop promised that he would ordain him a monk, according to their request.

During the Vespers of the Feast of the Cross (17 Tut), after the prayer of the Psalms of Vespers, in the Church of St Mary, Bishop Theophilus initiated the ordination rite of Brother Shawky as a monk with the name Matta El Suriany (Matthew). On the morning of the Feast of the Cross, Tuesday 27/09/1949, after the Matin Prayers, Bishop Theophilus completed the ordination of Brother Shawky Hanna Allah as a monk in the monastery of El Surian with the name Matta El Suriany.

Comment:

Fr Mettaous was born on the feast of St Matthew the Evangelist, so it was no coincidence that he took on the name Matta for his monasticism! And do you know that the name Matthew means "the gift of God"? Let us stop here and contemplate on this miraculous choice of his name. It is as if he was prophesying of what God was about to grant to the Church and to monasticism in general - and especially to the Monastery of El Surian - an endless blessing through this monk. A little lamp buried under the basket of the wilderness! Everyone who knew him and interacted with him felt the overflowing grace and blessing of God that filled this holy man.

Fr Mettaous applied what is written in the Bible: "Thanks be to God for His unspeakable free gift." (2 Corinthians 9:1)

His First Days:

"Being much more a zealot of the traditions of my fathers." (Galatians 1:14)

Fr Matta's ordination as a monk was a point of spiritual increase, for since the first day as a monk he lived a serious and strict monastic life. He enjoyed sitting in his cell, and he would not leave it unless there was a job to be done for the monastery, of which we will explain later on in more detail, or to join in prayer of the Sunset and Midnight Prayers, which had a special place in his heart, for he was always careful to pray them continuously.

Most of the time he spent in his cell was dedicated to fulfilling his monastic canon and doing monastic handiwork. He excelled in copying old monastic manuscripts, which narrated of the stories of other monastic fathers and their prominent sayings.

His love of his cell might have been the reason for his excellence in all his spiritual gifts. It might have been the reason for him to explore the depth and height of the love of God. The love of his cell might have been the reason behind his famous saying: "the cell feeds the community, and the community fills the cell, and both of them complete the other."

His Work in the Monastery:

"I know your works and your labor and your patience...you have borne, and have patience, and for My name's sake you have labored and have not fainted." (Revelations 2: 2-3)

After his ordination as a monk, he was assigned the job of tending to the church, and cleaning it and keeping the supply of candles and sacred wine sufficient . He was also responsible for preparing the church for its various occasions. He was also in charge of the oil lamps, as in changing the wicks and filling the oil lamps, and lighting it.

In the year 1955 AD, the late Metropolitan Benjamin of El Monofia visited the monastery. After he had returned to his dwelling place, he wrote a letter of admiration of what he had seen in the monastery that was brought to his attention when he visited.

From the many things that impressed him, which was written in the letter, was the neatness and cleanness of the church, including the lighting of all the candles in the church. The following is what he wrote in his letter: "His care to light the candles of the church is a matter to be remembered for and to be applauded." "The works that I do in My Father's name, they bear witness of Me." (John 10:25)

Bishop Macarius the Ethiopian, the General Bishop, who used to live in the El Surian Monastery in the 1950's with the name Fr Botrous El Suriany, also recounts an incident when Fr Mettaous was in charge of taking care of the church. He used to dust the church, and then collect the dust and take it to the monastery garden to spread it around the garden. This was done for two reasons: the first being that the dust from the church is a blessing, so it is good to put it on fertile land to bless it. The other reason is that the dust from church is blessed and is not fit to be put in the rubbish with other wastes.

Let us contemplate, my brethren, on this heightened spiritual level, to the extent of paying attention to the minute details without excessiveness.

From his interesting accounts of his past life in the monastery, Fr Mettaous recounts how he used to sweep the old church from door to door and then wash the floor. He used to do this with the late monk Youssef El Suriany, who used to tease him sometimes saying: " Take it easy, the monastery will get soaked!"

It is important to know that the size of the old church was 146 meters by 45 meters and he used a simple broom made of palm tree leaves and an old can of water to bring water to wash the floor. He was not assigned this job of cleaning the church, but he did it out of his zealous love for the church. He reminds us of what the Psalmist said: "For the zeal of Your house has eaten Me up." (Psalm 69:9)

His Ordination as a Priest:

"And no man takes this honor to himself, but he who is called of God, as Aaron was." (Hebrews 5:4)

Fr Mettaous truly had the idealistic monastic attitude with all its teachings, and he was determined that he would escape any priesthood ranks, even if it drove him to escape from the monastery. After he spent about seven or eight months in the monastery as a monk, he was surprised one day that his Father of Confession, the late Fr Sidarous the Elder, told him to start memorising the Holy Liturgy because Bishop Theophilus was going to ordain him a priest soon. With great monastic respect, he revealed his intention not to become a priest and he begged him to tell Bishop Theophilus of his request to be excused. At this point, Fr Sidarous replied calmly saying: " Fine, my brother, pretend I never told you anything."

Saint Isaac the Syrian in truth once said: " Whoever runs after honour, it will run away from him, and whoever flees from honour, it will run after him and point others to him."

We leave this story to our beloved father to tell, after he was ordained a priest - unwillingly - at the hands of Bishop Theophilus, the Bishop of the Monastery. They played a little trick that is widely known about him!

"On the evening of 22/10/1950, as it is the nature of my job to clean the entrance of the church of St Mary in the El Surian monastery, there sat one of the elders, the late Fr Benjamin the great, across from the entrance of the church. He said to me: "By the way, Fr Matta, they say there is an ordination of a priest today!" So I replied saying: "Trust me, Father, calling comes to those who flee from it!"

After the prayer of the Psalms of Vespers, Bishop Theophilus stood up at the door of the altar. Standing in front of him were Fr Makary El Suriany (the late Bishop Samuel, the Bishop of General Services and Fr Hilasiasius the Ethiopian. Bishop Theophilus initiated the ordination of these two monks as priests. At this time, I was standing at the back of the church and I saw Bishop Theophilus pointing to me to come forward to him. I thought he wanted to ask me about something concerning the church, so I went to him. When I reached the door of the altar, I was surprised to see Bishop Theophilus putting his hands on my head and initiating the ordination of myself as a priest.

I was taken by surprise and I struggled to escape from his grip, apologising about not taking the new rank, but he was determined not to let go of me and so he did not accept my excuses. I had to submit in order to keep my vow of obedience and because of his high rank and so I accepted. Thus, I was ordained a priest on the morning of Sunday 22/10/1950, which is the 12th of Babah – the feast of the martyrdom of St Matthew the Evangelist.

The reason behind changing his name from Fr Matta to Fr Mettaous:

"Their bodies were buried in peace, and their name lives to all generations." (Joshua Son of Sirach 44:14)

At the beginning of the year 1951 AD, in March, the monk Fr Matta El Samuely (the late Fr Matthew the Poor) came to live in the monastery of El Surian. He was sent by Very Rev Fr Mina El Baramousy (the late Pope Kyrillos the sixth) from St Samuel the Confessors' Monastery, after the Holy Synod of the time removed him due to some complications.

When the late Bishop Theophilus wanted to change these monks last names (to change the residency of a monk from one monastery to another) for the monk Matta El Samuely. He wanted to change his name due to the fact that there was another monk in the same monastery with the same name. It is a general rule that there cannot be two monks with the same name in the same monastery, in order to avoid confusion. However, Fr Matta El Samuely refused to change his name, saying: "I am a Coptic monk and not a Syrian one!" He asked to be named "Matthew the Poor", (Fr. Matta El Maskeen) taking the name of Pope Mettaous the First (the 87th Pope), due to his good reputation and the fact that the monastery took care to print and publish his story. It was also revealed to him by Divine revelation that he should take up this name. In order to avoid confusion, Bishop Theophilus and all the monks from that day began calling Fr Matta El Suriany by the name Fr Mettaous, that is, they called him by the Greek name of Matthew.

Whenever Fr Matthew the Poor remembered this incident, he would marvel at the humility of Fr Mettaous, who humbly gave up his name, even though he was ordained a priest by that same name, Matta.

His ordination as a Hegumen and joining the monastic theological college in Helwan:

"Nor do they light a lamp and put it under a basket, but on a lampstand, and it gives light to all who are in the house." (Matthew 5:15)

Thus, Fr Mettaous lived a serious monastic life from day one and was a true example of an energetic and committed monk. He loved his cell dearly and he was very honest in all jobs assigned to him, being very meticulous to details. When Bishop Theophilus saw many of these good virtues in him, he wanted to make him run errands around the monastery, so he sent him to the monastic Theological College in Helwan. He later ordained him as a Hegumen on Sunday 7/10/1951.

The main purpose behind Fr Mettaous going to the Theological College was to educate him about the various church teachings. When Bishop Theophilus surprised him by telling him to get his bag ready to go to Helwan to the Theological College, Fr Mettaous tried to excuse himself by saying that he loves the monastery and has strong ties to his cell and would rather stay in the monastery. However, under the persistence of Bishop Theophilus and to be obedient, he agreed. He prepared a few things from his cell and stood in tears, farewelling his cell and hoping to see it again as soon as possible.

Fr Mettaous was accompanied by Bishop Theophilus on their trip to Cairo and from there to Helwan to reach the Theological College. On their way, Fr Mettaous was praying like his Lord, saying: "Nevertheless not My will, but Yours, be done." (Luke 22:42)

A Diligent Monk

The late righteous Very Rev Fr Mikhaiel Mina El Baramousy was the Dean of the Theological College at that time, and he was responsible for it. Bishop Theophilus asked Very Rev Fr Mikhaiel to take special care of Fr Mettaous and he was placed in the third year of the course (that was five years in total). Along with this, Bishop Theophilus requested that Very Rev Fr Mikhaiel make sure he was as good as Fr Angelos El Maharaky (Metropolitan Maximus of El Kaliobeya), because he was well known for being the abbot of the Monastery of St Mary in El Maharak.

Fr Mettaous was well known and loved by all the fellow colleagues of his class. He was studying in the same class with a team of great monks, amongst whom were; Fr Timothy El Makary (the late Bishop Timothy, the General Bishop), Fr Boules El Baramousy (the late Bishop Macarius of Kenna), the late Fr Mancarius El Mahraky the Great, the late Fr Maximos El Suriany the Great.

What is important to mention here is that Fr Mettaous was confessing with Very Rev Fr Mina El Baramous the Ascetic (the late blessed Pope Kyrillos the Sixth). Fr Mettaous was a role model of the hardworking student and a strict monk in his worship, following the correct monastic life.

When the Christmas holidays came, all the monks returned to their monasteries to spend the holidays among their brothers. When the holidays were over, all monks returned to the Theological College, except for Fr Mettaous, who refused to go back to the college. His love for the monastery and life of solitude and peace was such a powerful motivation for him to stay in the monastery. Whenever Bishop Theophilus saw Fr Mettaous, he would approach him and ask him "Father, why aren't you back in the College? Fr Mikhaiel is asking me about you!" After a long time of persistence, Fr Mettaous finally answered and said to him "My father, I came

35

to the monastery to be a monk, and not to be a student at school!"

And thus he stayed in the monastery, in the bosom of his cell, which he loved greatly.

His appointment as the Abbot of the Monastery:

"For if I do this willingly, I have a reward, but if against my will, I have been entrusted with a stewardship." (1 Corinthians 9:17)

After Fr Mettaous's return from the Theological College, he remained in his cell in the monastery and returned to his old job as the keeper of the church. He continued his work from the beginning of 1952 till August of 1955 AD.

Because Fr Mettaous had a strong personality and the fact that Bishop Theophilus trusted him, he appointed him as the Abbot of the Monastery. He was to take care of all internal affairs of the monastery, such as food, drink, clothing and tending to the needs of other monks. He carried on the load of this responsibility with all love and humility, and completed all its aspects with a joyful heart.

Fr Mettaous was displeased with the workload of being an abbot, because it disrupted his quiet and peace, which were his way of life and the motive to become a monk. And So, he handed in his resignation from the rank of abbot, which was in January of 1956 AD.

His journey to St Samuel's Monastery with a group of monks on Friday 20/7/1956:

"The earth is the LORD's, and all its fullness, the world and those who dwell therein." (Psalm 24:1)

After Fr Mettaous had resigned from being the Abbot, the position was vacant, but nobody wanted to fill the spot. This was in January of 1956 AD, right after the Feast of Nativity. Bishop Theophilus was angry. He remained in his cell, refusing to accept the congratulations of the Feast of the Nativity, until the fathers of the monastery chose a monk to fill the position of the Abbot of the Monastery.

At that time, Fr Matthew the Poor was living in a cell on the outskirts of the monastery. He came to the monastery to celebrate the Feast of Nativity. When he found out about the contention happening in the monastery and the absence of Bishop Theophilus, he expressed his full readiness to be the new Abbot. They informed Bishop Theophilus, who agreed and came out of his cell and celebrated the Feast with the other monks. Thus, the contention was resolved.

During the time when Fr Matthew the Poor was the Abbot of the Monastery, there grew a special bond between him and Fr Mettaous, until Fr Mettaous became a son to Fr Matthew the Poor in Confession.

The saying, "the wind blows against the will of the ships!", Is appropriate, for the peace that surrounded the monastery by the presence of Fr Matthew the Poor as the Abbot did not last long. A few contentions arose between him and Bishop Theophilus, based on matters concerning the tending of the monastery. These contentions are usually foreseeable in such circumstances and are usually resolved. However, these disagreements escalated and the situation spiralled out of control, leading to Fr Matthew the Poor leaving the monastery and going to Cairo to stay with Very Rev Fr Mina El Baramousy the Ascetic (the late Pope Kyrillos the Sixth).

The consequences of Fr Matthew the Poor leaving the monastery were significant, as ten monks left with him as he was their father of confession. On Friday 20/7/1956, ten monks left the monastery – among whom was Fr Mettaous El Suriany – and they headed towards the church of St Mina in Old Cairo, where they stayed with Fr Matthew the Poor.

Truth be told, Very Rev Fr Mina El Baramousy (Pope Kyrillos the Sixth) welcomed them warmly and tried to comfort them. They stayed with him for a few days.

It is mentioned that Bishop Theophilus tried to comfort the monks who left the monastery and promised them to do whatever they wanted, where possible. Bishop Sawiris also tried to mediate between these monks and Bishop Theophilus but all his attempts failed.

The ten monks insisted on not returning to the monastery. Instead, they agreed to go to the Monastery of St Samuel the Confessor in Mt Kalamoun. On Monday 30/07/1956, Fr Matta the Poor and the other ten monks got on the train heading to Maghagha and from there to the village called Zora. From there they headed to the Monastery of St Samuel the Confessor, where they stayed.

Fr Matta the Poor and his ten monks worked to renovate and refurbish the place that was poverty-stricken and lacked a lot of utilities at that time. The monks built some cells and planted vegetables and stayed in the monastery for three years. During those three years, Fr Mettaous led the Evening Agpia Prayers, Vespers and Midnight praises, as well as Holy Liturgies. He was a role model of the ascetic and honest monk.

He lived along some well-known monks at that time, including the late Monk Fr Andrawes El Samuely and the Late Monk Fr Saleeb El Samuely the Great. He mentioned to us that during his stay in the monastery, he experienced the most powerful and rejuvenating spiritual revival in his entire life, where he lived in complete solitude and quietness, away from any worldly materialism. However, he would realise his mistake, recognising that leaving the Monastery of El Surian to go to the Monastery of St Samuel was a blemish on his monastic history! It meant that he did not stay in the monastery where he was ordained a monk!

His return to the Monastery of El Surian:

"But the dove found no resting-place for the sole of her foot, and she returned into the ark to him." (Genesis 8: 9)

Due to the harsh way of life in the Monastery, and due to the high ascetic level which Fr Mettaous attained, his health began to worsen due to his extended ascetic fasting and physical struggles. He became very anaemic until the point where his feet were unable to carry him. He thought about going to his home town (in Kenna) where he would receive medical attention for his anaemia. He told his spiritual father Fr Matta the Poor about his idea, who quickly agreed to it, since he had known him a long time and had developed great trust in Fr Mettaous. Indeed, Fr Mettaous went down to the town of Kenna, which would have been his first time to visit his hometown after leaving it to become a monk.

After a period of recovery, he decided to pack his belongings and return to the Monastery of St Samuel, where his cell and brethren belonged but the Name of the Lord be glorified, and according to the prophecy of Isaiah: "It shall come to pass That before they call, I will answer; and while they are still speaking, I will hear" (Isaiah 65: 24)

At that time, Bishop Theophilus heard about the presence of Fr

Mettaous in the town of Kenna to seek medical assistance. Through his great fatherly love, he sought to speak to Fr Mettaous – through the assistance of Late Metropolitan Kyrillos of the town of Kenna – and he convinced him to return to back to the Monastery of El Surian.

Fr Mettaous was convinced, and so he packed his belongings. On 19/1/1959, Fr Mettaous returned to his beloved monastery in the holy desert of Scetes. Everybody, including the Abbot of the Monastery, accepted him with great joy. He went to his cell and found it exactly as he had left it.

Fr Mettaous returned to his old cell and his old duty as the church keeper (Kandaleft), as Bishop Theophilus promised him. He also assigned to him the duty of teaching the order of the Holy Liturgy to new priests. Among those new priests who received the order of the Holy Liturgy was Fr Bishoy Kamel. Thus, Fr Mettaous settled in his original monastery and into his cell.

Building his first cell on the outskirts of the Ancient Monastery's walls:

"A monk should purchase stillness to himself with all that he earns, even if this leads to a physical loss to himself" (The Paradise of the Monks)

As we previously mentioned, the first thing that surprised Fr Mettaous is the fact that all monks' cells are placed next to each other. He thought that each cell would be placed away from other cells. He yearned to have the opportunity to have a cell away from other monks' cells, in order to enjoy solitude and stillness. This thought stayed with him for a long time, until it was permitted by God.

In the year 1960 A.D. Bishop Theophilus began the demolition of the old group of cells that lay beside the ancient wall of the monastery, towards the western side. This was done in order that a new facility be built to accommodate monks in new cells. The person overseeing this project at that time was Fr Anthony of El Surian (Pope Shenouda III currently) and who was tied in a strong loving bond with Fr Mettaous at that time. They collected the remains of the demolished cell facility in order to use it to build a cell for Fr Mettaous – after seeking the permission of Bishop Theophilus.

In August of 1960, Fr Mettaous started building his cell, which was the first cell to be built outside the ancient walls of the monastery. His cell stood in between the Monasteries of El Surian and of St Bishoy. He continued working with simple tools that were present at his time, until he was able to finish it and live in it.

He remained in charge of church as a church keeper (Kandeleft), even though he lived outside the monastery walls. He would spend his daytime in his cell, then at evening he would go back to the church and do his work. Once he finished, he would stay in the cell allocated to him inside the monastery until the prayer of Midnight praises. Then he would return to his cell again.

To accommodate for his living outside the walls of the monastery, he was assigned the role of crushing wheat since the monastery used to make bread once a week, on Saturdays. He would come on Saturday and work at crushing wheat and making bread; then he would attend Vespers prayers and the Sunday Liturgy and then would return to his cell. He would then return to the monastery the following Saturday to do his job once again. This allowed him to stay in his cell the whole week without interruptions. It is true what the Wise Solomon said:, "And the desire of the righteous will be granted." (Proverbs 10: 24)

"I have a single path!

I loved it and lived in it!

Lived alone all this time!

I was in a community or a retreat alone!

Both suited me well!"
From the spiritual poems of Pope Shenouda III

The Story of the Three Trees:

"The wilderness and the wasteland shall be glad for them, and the desert shall rejoice and blossom as the rose" (Isaiah 35:1)

After Fr Mettaous had settled in his new cell outside the monastery, he decided to plant some vegetables such as rocket and parsley for the benefit of others as well as himself. Indeed, he started placing some pots containing the desired vegetables, taking care to water them regularly. To water the vegetables was a great and arduous job, since he used to walk close to one kilometre to carry two metal cans of water tied to a wooden stick, which he would place over his shoulders. He would fill those two cans a few times a week, in order to water the plants.

Despite this great deal of effort, the plants barely survived due to the extreme wind and temperature of the desert. One of the elderly monks advised him to plant trees instead, as they would provide the much needed shade and would act as a wind barrier to protect the cell from the heat of summer and the cold of winter. Fr Mettaous liked the idea and acted immediately to plant them.

The monastery at that time used to plant trees around the western water pump. Subsequently Fr Mettaous went to the abbot of that time, who was the Late Fr Aghathon El Suriany (who later became

Bishop Aghathon of the Diocese of Ismaelia) , to take permission to take some of the small tree to plant them. He received three trees.

On the way back to his cell, Fr Mettaous remembered a dream that his mother had 13 years ago before he became a monk in the monastery. She said that she saw Bishop Kyrillos – the former Bishop of Kenna – giving her three trees and telling her: "Give these to your son to plant in the monastery in which he will become a monk!" When Fr Mettaous remembered this dream, he praised God for this blessed revelation and His great sustenance to His beloved.

The three trees still stand tall in front of Fr Mettaous cell to this day. It has been close to fifty years since Fr Mettaous planted those trees.

Chapter 3

A Spiritual Guide and Mentor

Fr Mettaous as a spiritual guide and confession father:

"Let the elders who rule well be counted worthy of double honour, especially those who labour in the word and doctrine." (1 Timothy 5: 17)

Fr Mettaous was full of great virtues, such as the gift of guiding and soothing broken hearts, especially to those who were in great distress and need. An example below will clarify this virtue.

Once, a monk was in a great uproar and was furious. He came and sat down with Fr Mettaous and carefully listened to what Fr Mettaous was telling him until his soul was settled and he was calm and smiling by the time he walked out of the presence of Fr Mettaous. After this monk had gone, I went to Fr Mettaous and with great respect and asked him, "What do you do to these monks?! A monk comes to you in great distress and anger, and he leaves you in utter joy and relief." Fr Mettaous replied, "Look, father, the greatest mystery which God set in His Church is the mystery of repentance and confession, and so relieving a burdened soul is not an easy task."

From his great sayings about confession fathers and about confession in general:

- You have a confession father available all the time, and you can find one anywhere you go!
- The door to my heart and my cell is always open to you day and night and at any time you feel burdened, come to me!
- The confession father is like a garbage bin, you come and

dump your garbage to him and leave a clean man!

• The confession father is like a secure safe where you put all your secrets!

The beginning of his service as a confession father started in the year 1955 – during the period when he used to be the abbot of the monastery. He took on this service at the request of Bishop Theophilus, who asked him to take the confession of the monks and the brothers that wanted to become monks. This was due to Bishop Theophilus' trust in the ability of Fr Mettaous as an honest and trustworthy man to take on such a burden. Fr Mettaous refused to accept this service, giving the reason that he was unworthy to be responsible for this great service. Finally, in the year 1965 – exactly ten years after refusing the offer – Fr Mettaous started taking confessions of monks in the monastery.

Some monks that Fr Mettaous was a confession father to included:

• Hegumen Paphnutius El Suriany (Currently Bishop Mettaous, Abbot of the El Surian Monastery)

• Hegumen Anastasy El Samuely

• The Late Hegumen Athanasius El Suriany

• The Late monk Fr Euagrius El Suriany

This progress continued to include many other monks and bishops from other monasteries, who came from all over Egypt to become his spiritual children. Moreover, some of those who confessed to Fr Mettaous were bishops and here is a short list of some of them, ranked in chronological order of their ordination:

1. Bishop Paphnutius of Samallout

2. Bishop Mettaous, Abbot of El Surian Monastery

3. Bishop Misael of Birmingham (England)

4. Bishop Antonious of Manfalout

5. Bishop Matthias of El Mahalah El Kobra

6. Bishop Daniel , General Bishop

7. Bishop Theophilus of the Red Sea

8. Bishop Samuel of Shebeen El Kanater (Deceased)

9. Bishop Yousef of the Southern United States

10. Bishop Sarabamoun of Atbara and Om derman (Sudan)

11. Bishop Barnaba of Torino and Rome (Italy)

12. Bishop Martiros, General Bishop

Including these names above, there were other bishops who came from other monasteries, and also a large number of married priests too. Fr Mettaous continued to guide all his children – bishops, priests and monks – in the right path. He was a teacher, a guide, a mentor, and he prayed for them all.

He was a father to them all to the fullest extent. He would rejoice in their joys and would be upset for their mishaps and be pained by their suffering. He would try and ease their pains and carry their burdens with them.

On this note, we mention a memoir that was said by Pope Shenouda III on the golden jubilee of the monasticism of Fr Mettaous, celebrated on 23rd of September 1999, when he said:

"Whoever walks around the cell of Fr Mettaous, would find thousands and thousands of sins buried underneath the sand! One would also find a notice hung outside the door saying: 'Come to Me, all you who labour and are heavy laden, and I will give you rest.' "Fr Mettaous was a pure spring of spirituality that would not cease. He would give a word of benefit to one, a word of encouragement to another and a word of rebuke and remorse to another. He was faithful to implement the commands St Paul gave to his disciple St Timothy, when he said, 'Convince, rebuke, exhort, with all longsuffering and teaching.' (2 Timothy 4: 2)"

His qualities as a confession father

"Indeed I Myself will search for My sheep and seek them out. I will seek what was lost and bring back what was driven away, and will bind up the broken" (Ezekiel 34: 11, 16)

Firstly: His discernment and wisdom in his spiritual guidance

"The Spirit of the LORD shall rest upon Him, The Spirit of wisdom and understanding, The Spirit of counsel and might, The Spirit of knowledge and of the fear of the LORD." (Isaiah 11: 2)

Fr Mettaous El Suriany was gifted with wisdom and discernment in all spiritual matters; for his observations were always correct, his opinions very accurate and even his ability in foresight was always accurate.

Fr Mettaous never accepted the idea of believing in dreams and visions, even though he admitted that he received dreams and visions. However, he would never allow one of his children ever to get caught up in the thought of having dreams and visions. Maybe this incident can cast a light on how Fr Mettaous was strict and wise to refuse accepting dreams and visions and believing them.

One of the spiritual children of Fr Mettaous came to him and told him that he knew of a person from his University (third year Law degree in Banisweif) who said he had befriended St Abu Sefein. He said that the saint appeared to him in dreams and even spoke to him and walked with him to Church.

This person brought his friend to Fr Mettaous, who quickly warned him not to follow his dreams, as they were sent from the devil. He warned him that if he continued to walk in this path, he would be in great danger. However, this person did not heed to the advice of Fr Mettaous. Thus, Fr Mettaous said "Pray for him and may God protect him."

And indeed, it happened that this person walked down the wide gate and was lost in the world and its desires. He was the exact example of the saying in the Paradise of the Desert Fathers: "He who believes in dreams is likened to a person who follows his own shadow."

Secondly: His firmness and compassion

"For He bruises, but He binds up; He wounds, but His hands make whole." (Job 5: 18)

Fr Mettaous was widely known for his firmness and toughness with sinners, in order to bring them back to their senses and guide them on the right path.

But despite his toughness in confession, he was the example of complete and utter compassion and empathy, in a way that would seem conflicting to his firm nature.

Whenever one of his children would go through a rough situation, he would show all compassion and love to his child until the temptation passed by, and he returned back to safety.

He would also live the problems of others, even their insignificant problems and familiar issues.

Pope Shenouda III commented on this point on the celebration of the Golden Jubilee for the monasticism of Fr Mettaous on 23rd September 1999, saying:

"From Fr Mettaous' great love to his children, he would live the problems of others to the extent that he got diabetes and high blood pressure and other medical problems! So I asked the monks to ease up on Fr Mettaous to relieve him!!"

On this note, we mention a story that was told by one of Fr Mettaous' children, which clearly portrays Fr Mettaous' compassion and sensitivity, despite his firm nature:

"One time I was sitting down with Fr Mettaous, and I was confessing some spiritual mistakes, until I got emotional and started crying heavily. Fr Mettaous tried to calm me down but he could not. He could not bear my crying, so he stood up, and said: 'When you finish crying, call me. I cannot bear to see you like this.' He left me and went to his cell and closed the door. When I finished crying, I called him back and finished my confession."

'O mighty One who holds the whip in his hands and Your heart bleeds with tears.'

Thirdly: A balanced life

"The middle path has saved many." (The Paradise of the Monks)

The most important virtue that Fr Mettaous obtained was leading a balanced life between his personal life, as well as a confession father.

He was balanced in everything he did - in prayers, fasting,

prostrations, asceticism in general, in eating and clothing, and in spiritual guidance. When he would advise others to lead a balanced life, he would do so out of his own experiences in choosing extreme poverty.

This reminds us of what St Paul said: "Knowing, therefore, the terror of the Lord, we persuade men." (2 Corinthians 5: 11)

As we mentioned earlier, Fr Mettaous experienced extreme poverty and asceticism when he lived in the monastery of St Samuel the Confessor. He used to fast up to three days without food, along with numerous prostrations and ate food in only small amounts. He reached extreme poverty that deteriorated his health, and he was diagnosed with severe anaemia. This diagnosis forced him to return to his home town to receive medical attention.

When he spoke of balance, he was speaking out of an excellent experience which he survived and brought forth fruit for others to benefit from.

"I sent you to reap that for which you have not labored; others have labored, and you have entered into their labours." (John 4: 38) His resilience in the monastery, and refusing to go down to serve:

"Let each one remain in the same calling in which he was called." (1 Corinthians 7: 20)

We mentioned earlier how Fr Mettaous lived in the monastery of St Samuel the Confessor from 1956 to 1959. Also, this period of time was a period of great strength in his monastic life, from its spiritual and physical aspects in struggle and endurance. However, Fr Mettaous often would regret leaving his original monastery – the monastery of El Surian – even though he did not leave his monastery to go back to the world, but only went to another monastery. Despite this, his great love to El Surian monastery made him feel like he returned to the world.

The Throne of Jerusalem:

"Therefore when Jesus perceived that they were about to come and take Him by force to make Him king, He departed again to the mountain by Himself alone." (John 6: 15)

At the time of the enthronement of the Late Pope Kyrollos VI in 1959, the throne of Jerusalem became vacant (after the departure of Metropolitan Yacoubos from his throne) and so His Holiness desired to ordain another Metropolitan for the vacant episcopal seat.

His Holiness knew Fr Mettaous on a personal level as Fr Mettaous used to confess to him. His Holiness Pope Kyrollos VI informed Bishop Theophilus, the Abbot of the Monastery, of his choice of Fr Mettaous to be ordained a Metropolitan and Bishop Theophilus carried this message to Fr Mettaous. However, in all humility and real meekness, Fr Mettaous refused this elegant position and asked Bishop Theophilus to carry this message to Pope Kyrollos VI, saying: "Tell His Holiness that I am just a poor monk , who is not up to such responsibility and that I want to live and die as a monk in the monastery."And indeed Bishop Theophilus told Pope Kyrollos VI of Fr Mettaous' wishes, and His Holiness appreciated his desire to stay in the monastery.

The Diocese of Luxor, Esna and Aswan:

Nine years after Fr Mettaous was nominated as Metropolitan for Jerusalem, in 1968, some conflicts arose between the late Bishop Abram of Luxor, Esna and Aswan and some of the priests of the diocese. These conflicts were resolved by removing Bishop Abraam from the diocese, and so he lived in the dwelling of the monastery of St Anthony in Boosh.

At that time, Pope Kyrillos called for Fr Mettaous to come from his monastery and to attend to the conflict and try to resolve it, promising him that he would be ordained the new Bishop when the conflict was resolved. For the second time, Fr Mettaous ever so politely and humbly refused to take on that burden, reminding Pope Kyrillos how he refused to take on the burden last time, wanting only to stay in the monastery and to spend the rest of his life there. Pope Kyrillos pressed the matter on Fr Mettaous many times, but Fr Mettaous was persistent in his refusal and so he returned back to his beloved cell once again.

It is also worth mentioning that after the departure of Pope Kyrillos VI the Patriarchal Seat became vacant. During the elections for nominating a new patriarch, a few names were written down; names of people well known for their spirituality. Fr Mettaous' name was on this list of monks. This list was published in the "El Fedaa El Gadeed" (the New redemption) issue number 83 on Monday 19th April 1971, on 11th Baramouda 1687 of the Saints. But like his master, as it is written in the Gospel of Saint John: "And everyone went to his own house. But Jesus went to the Mount of Olives." (John 7: 53, 8: 1)

His goal was clear in his mind, which was never to depart from the monastery. It is mentioned that at one time, Bishop Theophilus asked Fr Mettaous to go to Cairo to serve there. Fr Mettaous went to Cairo only out of obedience but he did not last there long at all but rushed back to his monastery and his beloved cell and never left it again for any kind of service outside the monastery. He was steadfast in his goal, saying, "The monk is like a fish; he cannot live outside of water."

However, regarding his travelling to Cairo to receive medical attention, the incident raised a lot of eyebrows! In the final stages of his life, Fr Mettaous was violently ill to such an extent that forced him to go to Cairo to receive proper medical attention. This seldom happened and for this reason his health deteriorated fast during his presence in the monastery. The doctor taking care of Fr Mettaous, Dr Sherif Helmy, advised Fr Mettaous to go to the hospital in Cairo once a month to get proper medical attention and to do the mandatory pathology tests to ensure his good health. This was the advice from the caring nature of his doctor but what Fr Mettaous answered with was totally unexpected. He asked him saying, "You want me to leave the monastery every month! Do you want me to lose my monasticism?!"

When Fr Mettaous said that last sentence, he had spent about 54 years as a monk! This is more than half a century as a monk and yet he was still worried about losing his monasticism in the world, even if the reason for going back to the world was for his own health benefits.

It is to this extent that Fr Mettaous adhered to the most critical and minor details of a principle which he lived by his whole life, even through the pain of his many illnesses.

"Let us hear the conclusion of the whole matter" (Ecclesiastes 12: 13):

Fr Mettaous embodied the words of Our Lord Jesus Christ:, "But whoever does and teaches them, he shall be called great in the kingdom of heaven." (Matthew 5: 19)

He chose to live by the principle, which he lived to his last breath. This principle was to stay within the walls of the monastery and to strive in the monastic struggle. For this reason, we find him speaking about this principle with strength and passion, because he is talking out of sheer experience and not with empty words.

For this reason, his words had a great effect on their audience.

Bishop Mettaous , Abbot of the Monastery of El Surian, recalls that he once heard Fr Mettaous say: "I will thus live in the monastery, even if it were as the fiery furnace of Babel."

He lived and struggled in the monastery and therefore the Lord gave him an inheritance with the three youths who, "when they were brought up to receive glory in their bodies, the Lord came down and put out the fiery furnace, and it became as cold dew." (From the hymn Tenen)

He said that "Residing in the monastery is the safest and shortest path to Heaven."He walked in the pathway of his forefathers St Anthony and St Macarius and so the Lord blessed him with their inheritance, and he was crowned with their crown.

Chapter 4

Some of His Virtues
&
Personal Characteristics

St Peter the Apostle taught us in his second epistle how it is an invitation from God to walk in virtues; "As His divine power has given to us all things that pertain to life and godliness." (2 Peter 1: 3)

Thus there lies ahead of us a path of spiritual struggle, which we must venture through; "But also for this very reason, giving all diligence, add to your faith virtue, to virtue knowledge, to knowledge self-control, to self-control perseverance, to perseverance godliness..." (2 Peter 1: 5-11)

Dear Reader, as we explore the many virtues that adorned Fr Mettaous, we discover a garden full of flowers of varying colour and shape. All of these virtues give out a magnificent fragrance that fills all corners with its aroma. His monastic life was filled with virtues, some of which were obvious to everyone, but others were hidden. All of Fr Mettaous' virtues brought forth fruit after many struggles through sweat and blood.

The Paradise of the Monks teaches us, "Virtue wants from us only to obtain it alone." And thus Fr Mettaous sought every virtue with all his being and spiritual longing. Therefore, God gave him more abundantly according to his monastic yearnings.

"Tell me my brethren and fathers, where did our forefathers obtain their virtues? In the world or in the deserts? We shall never obtain those virtues unless we hunger and thirst, and live with wild beasts and die according to the flesh."

These memorable words that were spoken by St Macarius the Great were often in the mouth of Fr Mettaous, as he constantly reminded us and encouraged us with these words from his pure mouth. These words had a great momentum, only because he lived and experienced this advice until he was able to pour out his experience on others. Fr Mettaous virtues appeared not only in his words but also in his actions, and even in his way of thinking and his facial expressions.

He reminds us of the words spoken by our Lord Jesus Christ; "But whoever does and teaches them, he shall be called great in the kingdom of heaven." (Matthew 5: 19)

Now, dear reader, let us explore together, for our spiritual benefit, some of the virtues with which Fr Mettaous was adorned.

The virtue of Prayer and Spiritual Vigil:

- "Our Lord Jesus Christ went to the Mount of Olives, in order to fulfil His spiritual struggle with the Father in prayer. For prayer is the beginning and the continuation of the work. Thus, we do not ask for consolation placed outside the heart."

- "The main condition for an acceptable prayer to God is the purity of the soul from the pain of the old man, and the purity of the heart from sins, so that the person becomes a temple of God"

- "If it happened that you heard news and noise from the world through Satan, do not fear or be troubled, for before the noise reaches heaven, it is overpowered by a voice from the desert, which is the prayers of the saints and their pleadings."

These deep and highly spiritual contemplations about prayer, written by our beloved Fr Mettaous, are the product of his profound experience about the life of prayer. He lived this life of prayer, which is fit to be a curriculum and provides guidance in how to pray and its boundless power and its conditions for acceptance. He lived it and documented it, along with his contemplations, but he did not know that one day these contemplations would be uncovered as a priceless treasure.

When we try to talk about prayer in the life of Fr Mettaous, we tend to talk about him personally. He practiced prayer from all its facets, until it became impossible to differentiate between his life and his prayers. He lived a life of prayer until the saying of the Psalmist David fit him: "But I give myself to prayer." (Psalm 109: 4)

Fr Mettaous lived the life of prayer very simply and habitually. Before he became a paraplegic, as he used to move around in his cell, he never ceased praying. He used to pray a very short and simple prayer wherever he went: "Lord have mercy, O Lord save, O Lord rescue, the blessing of the Virgin and the Saints." He used to repeat this prayer hundreds of times without boredom or exhaustion.

Whenever we presented him with anything to eat, drink or wear, he would make the sign of the Cross on it and say: "Bless O my Lord Jesus Christ the Son of the living God, and repay O Lord those who tire for this." He prayed this prayer even for somebody who would offer him a cup of water. After he became a paraplegic and lost movement of the left side of his body, he would hold the cup in his right hand, and make the sign of the cross on it with his head. It is the power that cannot be limited by paralysis!

However, his spontaneity and simple prayers did not lack the required struggle and effort, for he was very specific about his spiritual life. He was prompt in his prayers and strict in his canonical prayers. Before he became very ill and bed-ridden, he would not sleep until the beginning of a new day and would then wake up and pray the midnight prayer and praise. When he used to get tired, he would sit down on a chair but would not sleep. If it happened that his eyes rested, he would quickly rise and wake up.

His feet were swollen many times because of his continual sitting down on a chair. One time he mentioned on passing: "We thank God, 35 years and we never let a psalm go!"

One of the fathers that lived near his cell tells us that he used to see the lights go on in Fr Mettaous' cell at the exact same time each day, to the extent that he said: "Anyone can adjust his watch to the light that turns on in Fr Mettaous' cell, when he would get up to pray the midnight prayers."

"When you pray, say: Our Father in heaven"
(Luke 9: 2)

This happened before the departure of Fr Mettaous to Heaven by about a year. When he had eaten dinner, he went to sleep, and I also went to sleep, after I made sure he was well.

At around one o'clock in the morning, I woke up to the voice of our beloved Fr Mettaous, who was awake and stared at the ceiling of the cell. I approached him and stood by him, observing the situation. He was so focussed that he did not even notice my presence in the room. Fr Mettaous was praying the "Our Father" very slowly and meaningfully. Every time he finished praying it; he would make the sign of the Cross over himself and then start again from the beginning. I stood there watching, mesmerised by this unique scene. After a while, I got tired, so I sat down and continued watching. This incident continued for more than two hours straight.

What could he be staring at so intently? Could his repetition of the Our Father be a form of prayer or ecstasy, or praise, or all of these things?!

We read about ecstasy as a very high level of asceticism, known by desert fathers who transcend beyond the level of "limits of prayer", but here we witnessed this phenomenon with our own eyes, in the life of Fr Mettaous.

From the inspirations of Fr Mettaous El Suriany:

Whosoever turns the pages of the book "The Orthodox Prayer Life", which was printed by El Surian Monastery (First Edition, 1952) they would see on page 4 an illustration of a monk with a long beard, standing upright, while praying with utmost reverence and submission to God, holding his hands to his chest and lifting his eyes up to heaven.

This illustration has a story...

During the time when Fr Matta the Poor was present in El Surian Monastery, in the 1950's, he went inside the church to pray in peace. He thought that nobody was in the church, but was surprised when he noticed Fr Mettaous standing the same way that was explained earlier.

Fr Matthew the poor was so astounded at this great sight of Fr Mettaous that he left the church and being inspired, and he went back to his cell and put down this illustration of the praying monk. He could not find a better illustration to decorate the book of "The Orthodox Prayer Life". It was a great example of the exemplary stature of a human standing before his Creator at the time of prayer.

It is true what the "Paradise of the Monks" says: "We are not in need of words, because words are copious in this age, but we are in need of works."

Bearing forth spiritual fruits:

Dear reader, we mentioned earlier how Fr Mettaous lived to the word the verse: "Men always ought to pray and not lose heart;... pray without ceasing." (Luke 18: 1, 1 Thessalonians 5: 17)

We would like to conclude this topic with a deep and spiritual conversation that occurred between Fr Mettaous the biographer.

It was one of the days of February 1994, when Fr Mettaous was well, despite his losing his sight, diabetes and high blood pressure. I asked him saying: "Fr Mettaous, do you get disgruntled by losing your sight? I mean, does it affect your spiritual life because it stops you from praying and reading the Holy Bible?!"

Fr Mettaous answered in a confident and joyous voice saying: "Not at all, I thank God, but I do not want to tell you," and he cut his sentence here, as if he were actually considering not telling me. I encouraged Fr Mettaous to reveal to me what he was about to say. So he continued, saying: "I thank God, but I do not want to tell you that, during this time of trials and illness, there was much more spiritual fruits, many times over than during the time of the initial struggle period!" If the spiritual fruit was plentiful during Fr Mettaous' wellbeing, compared to the initial period of struggle, how much more would be the spiritual fruits when every centimetre of Fr Mettaous' body was crying out in pain during his sickness? There is no doubt that his time was spent in unceasing prayers and praise to God, when Fr Mettaous was crucified with his illness in bed for twelve years, raising his eyes up to Heaven and his tongue and heart never ceasing in prayer.

Fasting and Asceticism:

"Take for yourself a medicine to your life, from the tables of those who fast, and revive your soul from its death." (St. Isaac the Syrian)

"Asceticism of the flesh is neediness, and asceticism of the soul is refusal of indulgence." (St Moses the Black)

Fasting is the first commandment given to man, when God told Adam not to eat from the Tree of Knowledge of Good and Evil (Genesis 2). In the past, many prophets fasted, and in the New Testament, Jesus Himself fasted and also His disciples, when the Groom was lifted from them (Matthew 9: 15).

All the holy saints and struggles, without exceptions, fasted to various degrees, and taught us that fasting and prayer are the two wings that allow the soul to soar high in the endless heaven of the spirit.

Fr Mettaous fasted to the highest degree. As we mentioned earlier, at the beginning of his monastic life, he used to fast for long times without food until his body became frail and weak. We also mentioned that, during his presence   at the Monastery of St Samuel (1956-1959) he used to fast so much, to the extent that his body became so frail and he had severe anaemia, which forced him to go to his home town to receive medical attention.

Due to his extensive knowledge of the higher degrees of fasting, he was moderate in his guidance to his children, especially in the matter of fasting.

However, asceticism is a life spent in more than one way and is explained in more than one meaning that is agreed upon. Each one of the holy saints explained asceticism as he lived and experienced it. It is the highest level of monastic virtues and is supported in the Holy Bible, "But seek first the kingdom of God and His righteousness, and all these things shall be added to you." (Matthew 6: 33) and St Paul taught it to us when he said: "And having food and clothing, with these we shall be content." (1 Timothy 6: 8). Fr Mettaous was ascetic in all aspects of his life, but he did so in wisdom and moderation, be it in food or clothing or sleep.

From the perspective of food, he had a famous saying: "The Holy Fifty days after the Resurrection is only a continuation of the Great Lent." This meant that the Holy Fifty days does not differ much from the days of the Great Lent from the life of asceticism, except for fasting and prostrations.

On this note also we recount a story of Fr Mettaous, when he would find nothing in his cell to eat. We leave the story for him to recount:

"The regulation of the monastery, which is still current, is that every Friday, a meal of lentils is cooked and distributed to all the monks. During these days, there were no fridges to keep the food from going off. So, I would take my portion of lentils and drain it using a clean piece of cloth, and then take little portions of the lentils and make it into little balls. I would set these balls in the sun to be completely dry and then keep them in the cell until the day would come when I would have no food to eat. I would take one of these dried balls of lentils, and put it in some hot water, and instantly it would turn into a quick lentil soup, which I would eat and thank God for it."

We also mentioned that Fr Mettaous used to sleep at midnight and then would wake up for the midnight prayers at 4:00am and stay awake until the morning. In fact, he used to sleep on a log of wood 10 cm high. He used to sleep on this log until he became partially paralysed, which forced him to sleep on a medicated bed. Also from the countless prostrations, the skin of his knees died and calloused.

A Total of 275 cents:

In the year 1969, Fr Matthew the Poor was accompanied by some monks to go to the monastery of the Great St Macarius, in order to restore its buildings. When Fr Mettaous knew of what Fr Matthew was doing, he wished to contribute to the work with some money. At that time, all he owned was 275 cents and so Fr Mettaous put the money in an envelope, along with a letter of encouragement and words of love. He sent the letter to Fr Matta by the hands of one of the workers at the monastery. This reminds us of the story of the widow that put in the two mites, for which the Lord magnified and praised her saying; "Assuredly, I say to you that this poor widow has put in more than all those who have given to the treasury; for they all put in out of their abundance, but she out of her poverty put in all that she had, her whole livelihood." (Mark 12: 43-44)

Have a seat on the sack:

Fr Mettaous' cell was far from lavish, for its floor was spread with straw, and you could only sit on the floor. One day Metropolitan Hedra of Aswan, who was also the Abbot of St Bakhomious Monastery, came and visited Fr Mettaous in his cell. Fr Mettaous received his guest with great honour and respect and the Metropolitan sat down on the straw. In the corner of the room, there lay an empty sack spread out as if it were prepared for the important guest. Fr Mettaous said to Metropolitan Hedra, "It is unacceptable for you to sit on the straw, your Grace, please have a seat on the sack!"

Is there anything else but this?!

One of the many facets of Fr Mettaous' asceticism is the fact that he only had one type of drink to offer to his guests, which was cold Fenugreek (Helba) and here is a nice story regarding this fact.

On the eve of the Liturgy for choosing the next Patriarch over the Sea of St Mark, after the departure of Pope Kyrollis VI, two of the three nominated monks came to visit Fr Mettaous in his cell. One of the monks was Bishop Shenouda, Bishop of Education (Currently Pope Shenouda III, may God prolong his years) and the other monk was Bishop Samuel of the General Services. Fr Mettaous welcomed them very dearly and wanted to offer them a drink, so he asked them; "What would you like to drink, fathers?" And so Bishop Shenouda looked at Bishop Samuel as he said to Fr Mettaous, "What would we drink! Of course Helba! Is there anything besides this?!" Everyone laughed in great and honest brotherly love.

Fr Mettaous used to jokingly call this drink, "the drink of the most distinguished guests".

Truly magnificent is the simple life, for "Indeed those who are gorgeously apparelled and live in luxury are in kings' courts." (Luke 7: 25), but, "Better is a dry morsel with quietness, than a house full of feasting with strife." (Proverbs 17: 1)

Humility:

"Many say that this person is humble, and that person is proud but why is this so? There is nobody who is humble but Jesus Christ the Incarnate God. If a man is characterised with this virtue (humility) then in my opinion it is not the true nature of mankind and how can dust be humble?! For this reason, a monk must remain unknown from everybody, where no glory nor praise nor care is directed to him. Only then will he be sure that his self is protected from the vain glory of this passing world." (Fr Mettaous El Suriany)

This is one of Fr Mettaous' contemplations, and its weight is reflected by Fr Mettaous' life. Although he was well known for his strong personality, seriousness, steadfastness, attention to details and courage in truth, (and it was said about him that he never feared the blame of anyone), yet he was a very humble man.

We cannot specify in which part of the life of Fr Mettaous humility occurred since his whole life was filled with it and for this reason also we cannot talk about his humility separately. However, we tried to compile incidences in his life, which show deep and true humility, not just "sounding brass or a clanging cymbal." (1 Corinthians 13: 1)

The Barber:

At the beginning of his monastic life, Fr Mettaous used to take the blessing of many services, among which was the blessing of "the barber of the monastery". Any monk that requested to have his hair cut or shaved would go to Fr Mettaous in his cell and the latter would do his job without complaining, frustration or arrogance. During the hair cut, Fr Mettaous would talk to the monk about the Holy Bible and the stories of the holy saints. He would not allow useless conversation to take place. After he finished his job, he would welcome the monk to a drink in his cell, after which the monk would leave the cell very enlightened and joyful.

Other examples:

Even though a big number of bishops confessed to him, we never heard him say "This is my son in confession." Whenever anyone would say that so and so is one of your sons in confession, he would quickly correct him saying: "Pardon me father, we are all children of Christ."

This is only a fraction of the many stories that depict Fr Mettaous' great humility. For a benefit, we mention this story of a monk who asked Fr Mettaous how to gain humility. He replied saying; "Humility is granted to those who serve others and appears in the dealings and friction between your brothers in the community." Simple words, and yet they reflect how deep his humility is. We will conclude this chapter with an excerpt from his writings about humility:

"Truly wonderful are the words that speak of humility; this virtue that was praised by all saints, who sought it with great effort. It is the cloak of Divinity that our Lord wore when He was incarnated and took the image of a servant. Humility is an endowment given to complete the other virtues, and it is also the bearer of other virtues. The more a monk descends into the depth of humility, the higher is his stature in such a virtue."
Rejection of praise and escaping vain glory:

"I do not receive honor from men... O Father, glorify Me together with Yourself." (John 4: 41, 17: 5)

Whoever knew Fr Mettaous closely would know this virtue in him; his extreme dislike of praise from others and vain glory. He used to get very upset, and sometimes would get angry when we praised him in any matter. He would quote this line from the Paradise of the Monks that says: "Do not praise a monk to his face, lest you deliver him to the hands of his enemies." He would always give God all glory and praise that he received, but he would never accept any of it to himself. He would blame himself and say; "It is all because of my sins." When we forcefully praised him he would reply in true modesty and humility saying; "What would God's judgment be?!"

Those who attended the Golden Jubilee for Fr Mettaous as a monk, have seen and heard the many appraisals of a multitude of people. However, he was deeply moved by these words...tears upon tears...it is the deepest and most accurate presentation of his heart that does not like the praise of others and his aversion towards words of admiration.

Fr Mettaous was very careful to limit the circle of his friends and that was due to his dislike of vain glory. Thus, he was working tirelessly to submit to the words of the Paradise of the Monks: "If you want to be known to God, make sure you are not known to people."

On this note, we recount the story of one of his beloved spiritual friends. One day he came to Fr Mettaous, along with his parents and siblings to receive his blessings. Fr Mettaous greeted them warmly and upon their departure he blessed them. Before they all left, Fr Mettaous called his friend aside and asked him saying: "What did you do? You brought me a whole trip?!" The brother replied: "Not at all, Father, they are only five or six people who wanted to receive your blessings." Here Fr Mettaous replied sternly saying: "My father, I only know five or six people in my life and you come bringing me all five or six at once!"

His fondness of silence:

"He who guards his mouth preserves his life." (Proverbs 13: 3)

Whoever has seen Fr Mettaous' cell from the inside, would have noticed that there are a number of verses written in nice handwriting and hanging on the walls of the cell. What captures one's attention most is that many of the verses speak of one topic, and that is silence. Some of these verses:

"Therefore the prudent keep silent at that time, for it is an evil time." (Amos 5: 13)

"Many have fallen by the edge of the sword, but not so many as have fallen because of the tongue." (Jesus Son of Sirach 28: 18)

Some of the desert fathers' sayings:

"If only words bring as much benefit as does silence." (St Gregory the Theologian)

"If you want to know a man of God, be guided by his continual silence."

"Whoever lets his tongue free to say good or evil on people, does not qualify for the Grace of God." (St. Isaac the Syrian)

It is a known custom for monks to hang up verses on their cells' walls, as well as some of the sayings of the desert fathers. Each monk would choose the topic that suits their own spiritual goal, and so it reflects their struggle in such a path and thus was Fr Mettaous. Out of his love of this virtue of silence, he wrote and hung sayings and verses that reflected how focussed he was about living this virtue as a monastic virtue.

Fr Mettaous was already known not to be a talkative person. Whenever he would talk, his words would be seasoned with verses from the Holy Bible and the sayings of the Desert Fathers. When the illnesses began to take hold of him, his words were significantly reduced. Fr Mettaous became a silent homily, instead of being a meticulous speaker. Even his few words were accurate, and they touched the hearts of many directly. This is an example of what St John Saba said; "Quieten your tongue so your heart can speak, quieten your heart so God can speak."

Obedience:

"Obedience is demonstrated vividly in the personality of our Lord Jesus Christ, who was obedient until death. Thus, man must also obey God and His commandments."

"Truth has taught me that it is more important to obey God than people because if I please people, I am no longer a servant of Christ." (Fr Mettaous El Suriany)

Obedience is one of the three vows of monasticism, which a monk vows on the day of his consecration. For a monk must live in total obedience to God, by obeying His commandments. Obedience must also be to rulers and higher authorities, as well as to the Spiritual confession father, who takes care of a monk's spiritual wellbeing. They say that obedience frees from responsibility.

Fr Mettaous was always encouraging us to obey and especially those of higher ranks and authorities. He wanted us to receive the blessing of obedience, for St Anthony the Great once said: "Let everybody give you blessing."

In his case, Fr Mettaous was very obedient in his daily life. He was obedient to his parents and when he joined the monastery, he remained obedient and grew in it. He was obedient to the rules of the monastery, as well as his personal rules and he was also obedient to the Abbot of the Monastery in everything he said, even if it contradicted his personal wishes. As we saw earlier, we witnessed how he refused to be ordained a priest, but when Bishop Theophilus put his hand on him, he obeyed. Also, when Bishop Theophilus asked him to join the Theological College of monks, he agreed to go out of obedience. However, he only stayed there for a few months before returning to his monastery, after receiving the blessing of obedience.

When he was given the order to go to the Ezbaweya (the dwelling of the monastery in Cairo) and he did not want to leave his monastery, he still obeyed. He quickly returned after achieving obedience, so that he may not miss out of the blessing of obedience.

In all truth, Fr Mettaous was obedient in everything, to the point that he embarrassed us, his little children. During his sickness, he was obedient to an amazing extent. His daily life and situations reflected how much he valued obedience, as we shall mention with a few stories.

For example, we would wake him up and so he would obey and wake up, even if he did not have enough sleep. He would not want to eat, so we tell him to eat and he would eat according to our will. He would ask for a quarter of a cup of water to drink and we ask him if he would rather have half a cup and he would obey and take half a cup, but would only drink half of what was offered him. If one of the fathers wanted to visit him, I would tell him "Fr Mettaous, see what so-and-so would like to drink." He would say "You ask him!" then I would reply "Father, this is your cell, you ask him." Then he would obey and ask the visitor what he wanted to drink. On many occasions, he would not want to recieve visitors or see anybody, but if we asked him to see somebody, he would obey and allow visitors according to our wishes. On many occasions also, when he was sick, we would ask him to go to Cairo to seek medical attention, but he would say "it is something minor that will go away on its own." However, when we insisted, he would agree and go to Cairo.

These minor incidents, though they seem unimportant and some might say they are only natural, yet they reflect the depth of Fr Mettaous' love to the virtue of obedience, and his utter struggle to attain it, even through his illness and major health issues that he faced. In summary, Fr Mettaous was very obedient, despite his high monastic level and expertise in monasticism for many decades.

Be obedient, Father:

On one of winter's cold days, I asked Fr Mettaous: "Today is the day for showering, are you ready, father?" He replied saying: "Not today, father because it is very cold." I replied with a joke saying: "Be obedient, father, and listen to me." And here Fr Mettaous answered in all humility and meekness: "Obedient!! Believe me, father, you will not find obedience more than this."

Go back to your cell, Father:

Bishop Theophilus, the Abbot of the Monastery of El Surian, tells us of an incident that happened with Fr Mettaous. Fr Mettaous was heading to his cell outside the monastery, when he walked by Bishop Theophilus, so the latter asked him: "Where are you going, Fr Mettaous?" So Fr Mettaous replied: "I am going back to my cell, father."

Bishop Theophilus then replied saying: "No, my son, do not go to your cell today, but instead stay with us in your cell inside the monastery." Fr Mettaous did not respond, but turned around and obeyed Bishop Theophilus and went back to the monastery without complaining.

When this incident happened, Fr Mettaous had been a monk for about thirty years and was a confession father to many other monks. Despite this, he obeyed out of the sake of obedience alone. This is the obedience that he lived personally before he taught it to us.

Faith and submission:

"O Lord, we are ashamed, and You are plenteous in mercy. May we disregard this passing world and this perishable body, and say to You my soul is in Your hands at all times, do whatever You will. I submit my will to You, O Lord, who bought me with Your honored and precious Blood."

"May the will of the Lord be done...whatever God brings is blessing and good...all things work together for good..."

These simple words were always in Fr Mettaous' mouth, repeating them frequently. They reveal the depth of his faith and submission and how he lived by them and with them.

Whenever we presented him with a certain situation or problem, whether it was spiritual or not, he would always give advice like a caring father and then conclude his advice with: "Pray and may the will of the Lord be done."

If we have a quick look at his life and the many rough stages he went through, we can notice a pattern of endurance and submission to the will of God with such faith. We saw how he left the world and sought monasticism and how he ended up going to the wrong monastery, El Surian, instead of St Samuel's Monastery. We witnessed his faith and submission to such an unexpected turn of events. Even after becoming a monk, he left St Samuel's monastery and went to El Surian monastery again. He passed through terrible illnesses with painful details. We saw him getting one illness on top of another and especially when he became quadraplegic, he always used to say it's a blessing. Such deep faith and unmatched submission to the perfect will of God.

One time, this great submission prompted me to ask Fr Mettaous saying: "Fr Mettaous, we give you medicine to take and you take it, we give you drink and you drink it, we tell you to open your mouth and eat such and such and you obey. You never complain or refuse, or even ask what medication we are giving you?!" Fr Mettaous replied with the innocence of children saying: "Because I have faith that you would never give me anything that would harm me."

If his faith in such little matters is so apparent, how much more is his faith in God and his submission to God in all spiritual aspects of his life. No doubt his faith was so strong and his submission courageous, as he has submitted his life to the hands of the Creator, remembering the saying of St Peter: "And who is he who will harm you if you become followers of what is good? But even if you should suffer for righteousness' sake, you are blessed. And do not be afraid of their threats, nor be troubled."" (1 Peter 3: 13-14)

And finally, I recall hearing Fr Mettaous repeating the words of the Psalmist so many times: "I have been young, and now am old; yet I have not seen the righteous forsaken, nor his descendants begging bread." (Psalm 37: 25) He used to get really touched by this verse and would shed tears that made him struggle to finish saying it, because he felt that this verse applied to him greatly.

Patience and endurance:

"Monasticism is the path of repentance, when we walk in this path, we do not revolt from it, but continue with patience until death. And when God sees our patience and endurance, He will speedily come to our refuge. Let us wait and be patient, and let us struggle with wisdom and understanding." (Fr Mettaous El Suriany)

These sayings, amongst others, depict the extent of Fr Mettaous' concern over the virtue of endurance and the need for patience.

There is nothing that more clearly resembles this to us than the life of Fr Mettaous himself, which was full of temptations, sadness, illnesses and pain. However, he endured them all with thanksgiving and waited patiently until he received his crown fully. If we were to match his character to a person from the Holy Bible, there is nobody better to choose than Job, the Righteous. Truly he deserves to be called Job of the New Testament. We quote some verses such as: "that man was blameless and upright" (Job 1: 1), " Behold, happy is the man whom God corrects; Therefore do not despise the chastening of the Almighty." (Job 5: 17), "Now the Lord blessed the latter days of Job more than his beginning" (Job 42: 12)

Despite all that he went through, Fr Mettaous was never seen to grumble or complain about his various illnesses and pains, but we saw him endure with amazing silence and his face was emanating with peace and joy that reflected on those around him.

Who would have thought that a human being who is blind and paraplegic, bound to his bed for so many years and stricken with a multitude of diseases, would not complain or even groan a bit?!

How was he not stricken with boredom? Or maybe he struck boredom to death and so it fled from him and never came back. It is patience and endurance which cannot be physically attained. It is the Divine Grace that assisted him and so he struggled and conquered.

The patience and endurance of Fr Mettaous was not strictly in regards to his life alone, but it extended to include others as well. Many of his spiritual sons who confessed to him also endured a lot with him. He endured their weaknesses, struggles, problems and burdens and he had a famous line: "My tongue dissolves until one of you wears a black garment!"

I remember I saw Fr Mettaous staying up and so I asked him, "Why are you still awake and did not go to sleep yet?" He answered and said to me, "I'm burdened with your burdens! If one of you complains about a headache, I cannot sleep at night." This shows to what extent Fr Mettaous carried the burden of others.

Fr Mettaous confided in one of his spiritual sons in monasticism, during a spiritual gathering, "I thank God that I only got a Cross from Monasticism!" But every Cross is proceeded by Resurrection and every pain is crowned with glory.

Love and Peace:

"As for love, which is the level of perfection, there is no greater love than for a man to lay down his life for those whom he loves. For God so loved the world that He gave His Only Begotten Son. For God is Love." (Fr Mettaous El Suriany)

Human love consists of three major categories, which are the love of man to God, the love of man to his brother, and the love of man to himself.

The Lord Christ taught us that the love of man to God and the love of man to his brother are the two most fundamental commandments and on which hang all the Law and the Prophets. (Matt 22: 40)

However, the love of man to himself is for a man to work out his own salvation, even if it means the destruction of his physical body (Mark 8: 35-37).

Thus was Fr Mettaous; he loved God with all his heart when he turned his back on the world and departed for the desert to offer his life as a sacrifice of love to God, Whom he loved more than anyone or anything else. This divine love remained kindled during all the years of his monasticism, until he departed from this world to meet with his Groom and to live this love in its most complete manner.

Since monasticism is death from the world, Fr Mettaous walked the path of monasticism as a path to salvation, even if it were in return for his physical health. However, he set his sights on the saying of the Lord Christ, "Whoever desires to save his life will lose it, but whoever loses his life for My sake will save it." (Luke 9: 24)

And thus Fr Mettaous loved his soul with a true love and labored to save it from the prison of this world and its ties.

On the other hand, his love to others was no secret but it was so obvious to everybody. Out of his tremendous love, he cared about everything that pertained to everybody, regardless of how insignificant it might be. If he ever found out that one of his loved ones was passing through tough times or tribulations, he would not stop enquiring about them, praying about them and sometimes even deeply touched to the extent of crying for them.

It has been said about Fr Mettaous that when one of the brethren wishing to become a monk asked him what was the greatest virtue in monasticism, that Fr Mettaous replied and said, "Love and humility." He would then comment about love being the greatest of all virtues and the foundation of all other virtues. If we were in his presence, we would ask him and say: "Which virtue is the greatest?" he would always reply, "Love."

"Take heed that you do not despise one of these little ones, for I say to you that in heaven their angels always see the face of My Father who is in heaven." (Matt 18: 10)

Fr Mettaous always used to warmly welcome novices seeking

monasticism. They would visit him in his cell and he would welcome them with great friendship and love and give them encouraging advice and guidance.

We recount a story of one of the brothers seeking monasticism who was a spiritual son to Fr Mettaous. He suffered a great deal of back pain, upon which the doctors advised him to lie on his back for three months until his condition settles down. Out of his great love, Fr Mettaous would go and visit this brother personally to check up on his condition and to receive his confession. Just to remind the reader that Fr Mettaous suffered a great deal of pain personally at that stage and was also crippled by his blindness.

Fr Mettaous had the love that sacrifices and the true fatherhood, about which the Lord reminds us in the book of Ezekiel, saying: "Indeed I Myself will search for My sheep and seek them out. As a shepherd seeks out his flock on the day he is among his scattered sheep" (Eze 34: 11-12)

From the very spiritual and insightful rituals of those seeking monasticism, that on the night before being ordained as monks, these brothers would stay up the whole night praying inside the church. They would intercede to God to accept their monasticism and strengthen them in their struggle. They would also contemplate the new life that they were about to start and live.

Out of his love for these novices and when he was still healthy, he would stay up with the brothers and strengthen them, encouraging them with advice and guiding them in their spiritual path. When a father stays up with his children, there is no doubt that it leaves a great impression in the children, which they would always remember.

One of these nights witnessed the presence of the monk Touma El Souriany (Currently Metropolitan Bishoy of Kafr El Sheikh,

Dumiat and El-Barary, and the secretary of the Holy Synod, and the Abbot of the Monastery of St Demiana in El-Barary). Our beloved Fr Mettaous came to this special occasion and spoke to the brothers from the Bible and the sayings of the desert fathers. He said that night, "The Cell feeds the community, and the community feeds the cell, and each completes the other." His Eminence was very pleased with this saying, and he cherished it dearly. It is the experience of many years of struggle, which a father passes down to his children to benefit from it.

Fr Mettaous was also filled with amazing peace, which overflowed onto others around him. Whoever saw him would be deeply moved by his peace and joy, which would shine from his face, to the extent that they would find an excuse to visit our beloved Fr Mettaous just to see the joy and peace in him. They would not want to leave him. It is also amazing how many people who were hurt or in despair would visit Fr Mettaous and exit with such peace and comfort, just from looking at his face. It is as Saint Joseph said to Saint Anthony, "It is enough that we look at your face, our father."

The most important characteristics of our beloved Fr Mettaous:

"Until the day breaks And the shadows flee away, I will go my way to the mountain of myrrh and to the hill of frankincense. You are all fair, my love, And there is no spot in you." (Songs of Solomon 4: 6-7)

In the Christian perspective, a complete character is a character that is in harmony that is, there is harmony between its individual constituents and its external attributes. It is complete when the whole nature of a man is complete from all its spiritual, mental, physical and social aspects. It would be impressionable in the souls of others, through the work of the Holy Spirit who abides in him, through his actions and words.

In regards to Fr Mettaous, we witness his character not only through his actions and words, but even by looking at him or being in his presence. We recount to you this following story:

One day a worker came to visit Fr Mettaous to ask him to pray for him regarding his compulsory military service. After Fr Mettaous had prayed for him, the worker walked outside and was very glad and joyful. A monk walking by stopped the worker and asked him, "Did you visit Fr Mettaous and ask him to pray for you?" The worker replied, "Yes, but when I walked in and saw his face, I just forgot what I wanted to ask him. Do you know, father, whoever sees Fr Mettaous cannot go out and commit sin again!"

This is Fr Mettaous, who had an unusual effect on others around him, to whoever sees him, even to a simple worker.

We are not saying that Fr Mettaous was a perfect man, for perfection is for God alone, for we all know that everybody has flaws and nobody is perfect. We mean here the relative perfection for which everybody seeks to attain. There is a difference between perfection and seeking to attain perfection.

Whenever we would think that we are falling short of our goals in monasticism to attain perfection, feeling that we are not struggling enough and seeing that there is a bigger gap between where we are and where we want to be, Fr Mettaous would always reply and say, "If you want to be perfect, what is God going to add to make you perfect?!"

Here, we would like to cast a light on some of the most important characteristics that identify Fr Mettaous.

Organisation and Cleanness:

"Let all things be done decently and in order." (1 Cor 14: 40)

Cleanliness and organisation were two of the most fundamental characteristics in Fr Mettaous. He embraced these values and tried to apply them in his own personal life, calling that cleanliness and organisation should not interfere with the life of holiness, asceticism and dying to materialistic issues, always quoting the saying of St Paul: "Let all things be done decently and in order." (1 Cor 14: 40)

Fr Mettaous used to love cleanliness so much that it reflected in his life in all aspects. The way he dressed, the way he ate and even his cell was an example of a perfectly organised cell, despite it being nearly empty.

At this stage, we recount what Fr Matthew the Poor said regarding Fr Mettaous: "When one enters the cell of Fr Mettaous, he really enjoys serenity from its peace, organisation, cleanliness and simplicity."

Cleanliness was an integral value for Fr Mettaous, not only to him alone, but to anything that he touched with his blessed hands. We remind you here that when he was the "Church Kandeleft" (taking care of the cleanliness of the Church), he used to take care of its cleanliness to the extent that it caught the attention of visitors and even Metropolitan Benyamin noticed it, as we previously mentioned. When he was also given the service of cleaning the monastery, he used to sweep and spray the floor as we also mentioned before.

One time, our beloved Fr Mettaous, mentions a story of how he used to take care of his own cleanliness. "In the beginning, there were not many facilities to use to clean my clothes. Whenever I wanted to wash my clothes, I would have to wash them with hot water. To heat the water, I had to light a fire, and to light a fire I had to collect wood for the fire, to heat a tin can that had water in it. Now that times are better, I used to go to the generator of the monastery, and use the cooling water to wash my clothes as this water used to be hot." This is the extent that Fr Mettaous had to go to in order to keep his cleanliness.

Other fathers also recount similar stories of how Fr Mettaous used to come to the baking place and quietly sit down and organise himself to cut the bread in equal portions that amazed other monks. When he used to finish cutting the bread, he would get up quietly and leave in the same manner that he entered with. He would not have any flour or batter on his clothes; no evidence that he was even in the baking place. Monks used to marvel so much at this!

Fr Mettaous used to adorn with elegance all aspects of his personal life. He used to eat at set times of the day and was very strict about when and how to eat his food. When he finished eating, he would not show any impressions regarding eating, despite his health issues from losing his sight and paraplegia.

If Fr Mettaous paid that much attention to cleanliness and order, how much further must he have been careful about his monastic life and the cleanliness of his heart and mind. He is a vessel that overflows with its contents!

Savings and financial delegations:

"He who gives, with liberality; he who leads, with diligence; he who shows mercy, with cheerfulness." (Rom 12: 8)

Fr Mettaous used to be very wise with his schemes in all aspects of his life, whether it be his spiritual or materialistic and he always used to utter the words taken from the Paradise of the Monks "As a wise sailor, contrive the ship of your life." He used to collect things that we thought were useless and we confronted him once and told him, "Father, these things are useless", and so he replied and said, "My fathers, we are in the desert, anything can be useful." He also used to say, "Whoever saves something, it is as if he earned it." Days go by, and we realised that the things that we objected about became useful later on.

One of the things that Fr Mettaous taught us from observing him is being content with your own rations (the share of each monk), which the monastery distributed to the monks. He would never ask for more, or buy anything extra to what he was given. He always used to say, "Keep your shares, for they are money for the poor."

The attributes of his personal life reflected in his external behaviour and so he would take special care of the monastery's property as if it were his own.

We recall that when Fr Mettaous was the abbot he used to pay attention to every minute detail and would take care of every property belonging to the monastery. The extent of his diligence and attention to detail was an example and role model for others.

We also recall an instance when Fr Matthew the poor spoke about Fr Mettaous regarding this matter: "One time I walked in on Fr Mettaous when he used to be the abbot and he had a large piece of paper spread on his desk. The piece of paper had little torn pieces from it, and so Fr Mettaous got sticky tape and was fixing the little tears in it. He had the authority to get more pieces of paper and discard the torn one, but he chose to preserve the monastery's property." This minor incident shed light on Fr Mettaous' characteristics, from honesty to humility, to simplicity, to financial delegations.

Finally, we would like to conclude this excerpt with a little piece of information, which might come as a surprise.

All the sayings which were recorded from Fr Mettaous, whether it was recorded in the second part of this book, or whether it was passed down and published in the book of the Golden Jubilee, or not published at all - (and which are so powerful and full of life experiences) - were not written down in journals or books, but rather on scrap pieces of paper. We went to a lot of trouble to dig out those snippets and compile them into this treasure for the benefit of others. It is the mustard seed "which indeed is the least of all the seeds; but when it is grown it is greater than the herbs and becomes a tree, so that the birds of the air come and nest in its branches." (Matt 13: 32)

His simplicity

"The simple people are the ones that hasten to accept the word of God with faith and simplicity, without examining, and so it is easy for their salvation. Their service is uncomplicated. By Your grace, give us to live in front of You all our lives with the simplicity of fishermen, that we may be worthy to be thrown in the Fatherly Bosom of Your exceptional love." (Fr Mettaous El Suriany)

Have you ever seen doves? You might have seen one flying in peace, or calmly sitting in a place, over its eggs, or singing in quietness and humility. Even when in crowds, it simply and quite. We saw all of these attributes hidden in the person of Fr Mettaous.

When the Lord Christ commanded us to be simple and harmless, he asked us to be "harmless as doves" (Matt 10:16), and this is what Fr Mettaous was!

Despite the reverence and awe that show in Fr Mettaous'

appearance, which is reflected by his looks and old age, when you get to deal with him, you find that he is such a harmless man, as simple as a little kid. You find that you are unable to not love and respect him at the same time.

Simplicity is the main characteristic of Fr Mettaous, whether it be in his words, actions or routines. His simplicity used to make him stand out, without diminishing his reverence. Simplicity was the slogan of his cell, but his simple words uncover a depth of hidden secrets. You ask him a question, and he responds in such depth and with such elegance that it fills the questioner with the right answer and fends away any disbelief or misunderstanding.

From the obvious aspects of his simplicity, Fr Mettaous used to get jubilant and satisfied over the littlest thing that we offer him, however simple it might have been.

Out of the love of other fathers to Fr Mettaous, they used to bring him any excess food or drink they might have. It might be as simple as a carton of juice, fresh fruit, or simple vegetables. He would accept them with love and heartly joy and simplicity of heart, saying: "May the Lord increase your good works, you didn't have to give me so much, God's abundance is overflowing." The giver would be so embarrassed by such love and would respond saying: "Forgive me, father, it is only a simple gift and I am embarrassed from you, father." Fr Mettaous would then respond and say: "May the Lord reward you, father, it came in the right time, and is so appreciated."

Despite the fact that he never embarrassed anyone who gave him gifts of any kind, but rather accepted it with love and simplicity, except that he would, at the same time, never ask anyone for anything, however badly he needed it. He would always say: "Thank God I am never in need of anything."

He often reminds us of the Apostolic Fathers who were gathered around the Lord on the night of the l Last Supper, when the Lord Christ asked them: "When I sent you without money bag, knapsack, and sandals, did you lack anything? So they said, Nothing." (Luke 22: 35)

Truly what more could he want when he has given up his life to Him who loved him, and had surrendered himself for Him (Galatians 2: 20)

Decency and reverence:

"On that day the Lord exalted Joshua in the sight of all Israel; and they feared him, as they had feared Moses, all the days of his life." (Joshua 4: 14)

Fr Mettaous was adorned with decency and reverence to a great extent. He lived out the saying of the Paradise of the Monks that says: "A light tread and a soft voice." He used to be very decent in his words, actions, appearance and even his walk. He never used to lean forward to joking around or laughing, but he always kept a serene, angelic smile on his face whatever the situation.

He used to say to us: "Through the grace of Christ we took up this path (monasticism) seriously and not mucking around." It is widely known about him that when he yawns, he doesn't open his mouth, and thus never shows his teeth, following the directions of the Paradise of the Desert Monks regarding that matter. However, this never stopped him from being quick witted. He would say a sincere and gentle joke if the situation called for it, or to calm down a rough situation.

We bring to you, Dear Reader, some of the stories that indicate the extent of reverence and decency, which others witnessed in his character

Ordaining the monk Bishay as a priest:

We previously mentioned that Fr Mettaous was once the abbot (the head of the monastery), in the year 1955. This year witnessed a great architectural revival and the engineer in charge of the projects was the monk Mousa El Suriany (who later on became Bishop Andrawes of Domiat and Kafr El Sheikh), since he was an engineer before being a monk.

During this time, Bishop Theophilus (the abbot of the monastery) wanted to reward Fr Mousa for his great efforts and so he wanted to ordain him as a priest. On one of the Sundays of September that year (1955), Bishop Theophilus was determined to ordain Fr Mousa as a priest. Fr Mettaous was present in the church at that time. So he went up to the Bishop and said to him: "Your Grace, we all love Fr Mousa and agree on him being ordained a priest, but, absolve me father, this does not replace the order of the next monk who was to be ordained a priest next! Your Grace will ordain Fr Bishay as a priest along with Fr Mousa."

Due to the great respect that the Bishop held for Fr Mettaous, he agreed to ordain Fr Bishay a priest also, as well as Fr Mousa and indeed it was carried out and everybody was at peace.

After shedding light on the great and mutual respect between Fr Mettaous and Bishop Theophilus, it is important to note that whenever Fr Mettaous went to greet Bishop Theophilus, His Grace would actually stand up to greet him, and would never be sitting down when greeting him. It is also important to note that Bishop Theophilus was older than Fr Mettaous and he was the one to ordain him both as a priest and hegumen. At that time, Fr Mettoaus had already lost his sight, but his respect preceded him in all situations.

Between the bBell of the Monastery of Abo Macar and the Bell of the Monastery of El Baramous:

It is widely known that, out of respect, the bells of the monastery are rung whenever the Pope, a metropolitan or a bishop visit the monastery, as a gesture of welcome.

It happened in the year 1978 that Fr Mettaous was on his way back from Cairo after he had run some tests for his health issues. He thought of passing by the monastery of Abo Macar to take blessing from the monastery and to visit the late Fr Matthew the Poor and the fellow monks.

When Fr Matthew the Poor was aware of Fr Mettaous' visit, he was very welcoming, to the extent that he ordered that the bells of the monastery be rung at his arrival, so that the other monks would come and greet Fr Mettaous and to take his blessings.

Also, in the year 1997, when Bishop Iciserous (Bishop of the monastery of St Mary in El Baramous) was going through some health problems of his own, Fr Mettaous decided to visit him, due to the great bond of respect and love between the two of them.

When Fr Mettaous approached the monastery, he found that Bishop Iciserous was standing at the gate, accompanied by a large number of monks, waiting to welcome him. When Bishop Iciserous saw Fr Mettaous approaching, he ordered that the bells of the monastery be rung as a gesture of welcome, but Fr Mettaous strongly refused the idea and with great effort he convinced Bishop Iciserous not to ring the bells, out of great respect between the two.

Promptness and thoroughness:

"See then that you walk circumspectly, not as fools but as wise, redeeming the time, because the days are evil." (Eph 5: 15-16)

Fr Mettaous lived by the two most important principals of his life, which were promptness and thoroughness. He was exceptionally prompt and very meticulous and careful in all aspects of his life. If he appointed a time or promised someone something, he delivered every time and on time. He used to teach us: "Promptness and thoroughness in the personal and physical life of a monk lead to promptness and thoroughness in the spiritual and monastic life."

We previously mentioned that Fr Mettaous was careful to wake up every night to pray. One of the father's comments: "If someone wants to set his watch, he can set it according to the cell of Fr Mettaous (revise The virtue of prayer and spiritual vigil)"

The life of our beloved father illuminates these characteristics. We present you, Dear Reader, some circumstances as examples.

God bless you father, you revise everything I do:

At the beginning of his monastic life, Fr Mettaous formed a close friendship with the late Hegumen Dimitri El Suriany the Elder (1950-1986). During this period, Fr Mettaous had a lot of services to attend to, but he often felt that he wronged somebody, or had fallen short in one of his services as a abbot. Despite his various errands and amid his busy life, he would always revise himself, lest he should have crossed somebody, or made somebody angry unintentionally.

This matter kept him on edge for a while, and so he went to Fr Dimitri and said, "God bless you father, you see that I go in and out of the monastery frequently and there are many errands I have to take care of and so I might act in a wrong way here or there. , Please, if you see me do anything wrong, or if I have acted wrongly, come and tell me and revise my actions."

He wanted to avoid being a stumbling block to others in the community and he desired to have a pure conscience without

91

blame. He did not want to have any misconstrued thoughts when he returned s to his cell, or when he stood before the altar. Is it true love or humility, or thoroughness, or a heightened spiritual sense, or a pure conscience regarding the little matters before the bigger matters? Or is it a combination of all these things?!

Wearing the Kolonsowa (Cowl):

It is known that Fr Mettaous was ordained a monk in 1949; thus the cowl he used to wear was different to the cowl that monks wear today.

The old cowl used to be a strip of black cloth of width 8cm and length 50cm, with crosses drawn on it. This is the cowl with which Fr Mettaous was ordained a monk.

However, when the church ordered that all monks wear the new cowl, with its well known design, Fr Mettaous was one of the very first people to obey the rule. He would never walk out of his cell without wearing the new cowl and whenever he left the monastery for treatment, he would wear the full monastic attire, despite the fact that the car that used to transport him would take him from door to door – or, in other words, from his cell to the hospital directly. Fr Mettaous lived the verse that says: "Have regard for good things in the sight of all men." (Rom 12: 17)

Fr Mettaous and accepting confessions:

When the Church issued a decree for monks not to take confessions from women, Fr Mettaous had only three women, from whom he was receiving confession. Each lady had a different story as to why Fr Mettaous agreed to take her confession, as an exception to the rule.

However, when Fr Mettaous received the news of the decree, he apologised with great respect to the three women and asked them to seek other priests, who   were   married, to take their confession. He did not want to hurt them emotionally by rejecting their confessions, but he explained that he must follow the Church decree in this matter.

One of these ladies knew His Holiness Pope Shenouda III – may God extend his life – on a personal level and so she went to him and said: "Fr Mettaous refused to take my confession, based upon the issued decree. But I have been confessing to Fr Mettaous for many years and am very comfortable with him." His Holiness issued her a special exception to confess to Fr Mettaous, due to his own personal knowledge of Fr Mettaous, and his utmost honesty.

Chapter 5

God's Work in His Life

Introduction:

When we speak of God's work in the life of Fr Mettaous, we merely speak of its revelations and some of its content, some of which are spiritual – and are beyond natural – and others are physical. All of these revelations took place in the years that we lived with Fr Mettaous.

Despite the fact that God was glorified greatly in His work with Fr Mettaous, yet Fr Mettaous was careful to hide all these matters, out of his love for humility and selflessness and also for the sake of escaping vain glory. He used to repeat the words, "I do not receive honour from men." (John 5: 41). He also wanted to lead us by example, not to seek after these matters as monks, so that we may avoid falling in the traps of the right-hand-side blows – may God protect us all from them!

What we saw is a great deal and it is rather difficult to gather and recount, but we will depict a sample of these recollections as examples only. God willing, we will present three major topics about his relationships with heaven and the heavenlies, his claivance and his miracles. It is a mere extrapolation for the unseen dimension of Fr Mettaous and an attempt to discover the depth of these revelations, which God entrusted in Fr Mettaous.

His Relationships with Heaven and the Heavenlies:

"Who established the ranks of the incorporeal among men. Who gave to those upon the earth the hymn of the Seraphim." (Gregorian Liturgy)

Despite his great bond with the heavenlies, he was very good at hiding this relationship, to the extent that he would become anxious to hide any such recollections of the times when the heaven was opened on earth. We would eagerly wait for the crumbs that fall off these spiritual tables, so that we might preserve them for our consolation and as treasures for the coming generations to uphold and from which to take an example. This was also considered as a reward for his struggles and a condolence for his great suffering in sickness.

In this section, we would like to present a few glimpses of such relationship with the heavenlies, including St Mary and the late Pope Kyrillos VI and how deep was his relationship with them and the great favour he obtained with them.

Fr Mettaous and St Mary:

Fr Mettaous enjoyed a close and personal relationship with St Mary and used to always ask for her intercessions and mention her name in any occasion, saying: "The peace of the Lord be on her, may she intercede for us." St Mary used to manifest to Fr Mettaous on several occasions, and he would describe her with the utmost precision and detail, such as her height, hair colour, colour of her clothes, and the head veil she used to wear. He would also recount the way she talked, and even the gestures she made while talking with him! Even though it was difficult for him to tell us about these revelations and what they talked about during such manifestations, he would, on occasion, surprise us with a recollection of some, but this would be after extensive begging, with the tone of fatherhood and love.

We present to you, dear reader, with some situations that show the strength and depth of such spiritual relationship that bonded him with our Mother Saint Mary.

I want you to go to the monastery tomorrow:

After the incidents that occurred in September of 1981 (i.e. the placing of pope shenouda under house arrest at St. Bishoy's monastery), security spread around the monastery of St Bishoy and El-Surian and visits to either monasteries were extremely difficult, as you would have to obtain a written approval from the Minister of Internal Affairs to enter these two monasteries.

During this hard time (1981-1985), two people went to visit His Holiness Pope Shenouda III in the   Monastery of St Bishoy. These two people were the late Hegumen Sarabamon Atia (from the church of St Mary in Ein Shams) and Lieutenant Dr Nepson Marcus. After they visited His Holiness and took his blessings, they visited the monasteries of St Bishoy and El-Surian, then returned to Cairo, having planned to return to visit His Holiness the following week.

After two days from the last visit, in the quietness of the night, St Mary appeared to Dr Nepson and said to him, "I want you to go to the monastery tomorrow!"

Dr Nepson woke up the following morning and called Hegumen Sarabamon and said to him, "I am going to the monastery today, would you like to come with me?" but he did not mention to him about the reason for this surprise visit. Hegumen Sarabamon was astounded, but he had to apologise because he was not ready for this sudden visit.

And so Dr Nepson prepared himself and went off to visit the monastery of St Bishoy first ,to visit His Holiness, but he was surprised to see His Holiness standing in front of the ancient church and around him gathered some of the monks of the monastery of El-Surian. Fr Mettaous had apparently entered a diabetic coma several hours ago and nobody had any idea of what to do, since they lacked sufficient medical apparatus, due to the extensive security around the monasteries.

His Holiness was troubled as he stood around with the rest of the monks, thinking of a way to get Fr Mettaous back to a healthy state.

And as they were discussing possible options, to their amazement, Dr Nepson arrived uninvited. After he greeted His Holiness and took his blessings, he was informed of Fr Mettaous' health deterioration.

Immediately, Dr Nepson asked to see Fr Mettaous and he was taken to the monastery of El-Surian with His Holiness, who wanted to make sure of his health. After a great deal of effort, Fr Mettaous finally awoke from the coma and His Holiness made sure he was alright and prayed for a healthy return. Fr Mettaous thanked His Holiness dearly for his concern and great love.

After this incident and through vouching from Dr Nepson, Fr Mettaous was granted the approval to leave for Cairo to seek medical attention. And indeed, Fr Mettaous went back with Dr Nepson to Cairo, and he accompanied Fr Mettaous during his period of care. During that time, he told Fr Mettaous of the incident that happened with him in his sleep, and how St Mary appeared to him. This happened at the same time that Fr Mettaous had fallen into that diabetic coma the night before.

This showed how St Mary cared for her beloved son Fr Mettaous and the extent to which she exercised that care, to send him a doctor with the exact medical expertise needed at such event. Indeed she is the essence of purity, generosity and blessings (The Priests' Absolution).

Fr Mettaous and Pope Kyrillos the Sixth:

We would like to remind you, Dear Reader, of the great relationship that attached both Fr Mettaous and Pope Kyrillos the Sixth with one another.

This relationship started in 1951, when Fr Mettaous went to the monks' Theological college in Helwan to spend a few months. During that time, he came to know of the monk Fr Mina the Ascetic (he later on became Pope Kyrillos the Sixth), who used to live in the Church of St Mina in El Zahraa. It is believed that this relationship was strengthened during this time, which allowed Pope Kyrillos to know Fr Mettaous' personality on a close and personal level.

The love that connected these two saints was a sheer spiritual relationship; fatherly care and guidance from Pope Kyrillos, and true and honest sonship from Fr Mettaous. This relationship started in the flesh but continued past this perishable world into the boundaries of Heaven, after the departure of Pope Kyrillos. For the Church teaches us in the Litany of the Departed "For there is no death for your servants, but merely a departure." When Pope Kyrillos departed, he merely changed his place of dwelling, but he remained on the same relationship with Fr Mettaous. This following story might confirm the truth of such allegations.

Early in 1998, Fr Mettaous was admitted to the hospital of Al Haya for treatment and close physical examination because he suffered a hardening of the aortic pump. During his presence in the hospital, his health deteriorated severely, as a result of a reduction in the ejection fraction of the heart to only 42%, instead of 51% when he was first admitted.

On 22/1/1998, at approximately 5 o'clock in the morning, Fr Mettaous asked me to help him to go to the toilet, because of the stroke which he suffered in 1996 and which caused him to be paraplegic on the left side. This is because, at that time he was unable to move alone without assistance, especially standing and walking! When he came out of the toilet, he asked me to sit him down on a chair, and so I did. I made sure that he was comfortable. Because I was physically exhausted from the day before, I thought of lying down on my bed until Fr Mettaous asked me to help him to sit on his bed too. However, I fell into deep sleep.

Suddenly, I was awoken with a massive jolt of anxiety when I saw Fr Mettaous standing at the door of the room, unassisted! This took me by surprise and from fear of Fr Mettaous being hurt by falling, I ran to him and embraced him. When he felt me, he said, "Did you wake up" he smiled and continued, "Now take me back to my bed." I took him back carefully to his bed, and was frantic to find out if he had injured himself during his move.

Questions swamped through my mind. How did Fr Mettaous get up from his chair and walk all this distance alone without help, despite the fact that he was paraplegic? How did he not hit any furniture in the room, despite the fact that he was blind?! How!

All these questions came to rest the following morning, when Fr Daniel El Suriany came and I recounted what had happened last night. We begged Fr Mettaous, with the favour of sonship and out of his love, to tell us how it happened? Who of the saints was with him the night before?

After refusing a lot, he finally gave in and said, "What is the big deal? Pope Kyrillos came to me; we had a little chat and then I saw him to the door. That is the whole story."

After I was alone with Fr Mettaous, I asked him, "What really happened, father?" He replied and said, "Pope Kyrillos came through from this balcony [and he pointed at the balcony] and went out of that door [and he pointed to the door]. I walked him to the door; then he left." I replied, "Why did you not wake me up, father, to take his blessings?!" Fr Mettaous replied, "My father, he was the one that woke you up!" At this point, I remembered why I felt a jolt through my body when I woke up.

I asked him again, "Please father, absolve me, but you do not see and have never been in this hospital before. How did you know the details of the room? How did you know that the balcony was here and the door was there? And how did you move around in the room to the door?" He replied with such a deep and insightful answer, which still rings in my ears till this day; he said, "My father, the world of the Spirit – never ask about it!

God continued His work, for through the blessing of this spiritual Papal visit, the health status of Fr Mettaous dramatically improved. An echocardiogram (ECG) was performed on him, which showed a great increase in the capacity of his heart's function. Due to this, Fr Mettaous was able to return to his monastery, in full health.

While we are still speaking about the special bond that tied Fr Mettaous with Pope Kyrillos, we recount the fact that, after the departure of Pope Kyrillos and while Fr Mettaous used to open his Agpia to pray – he would see the picture of Pope Kyrillos on the first page inside the cover of the Agpia. Every time Fr Mettaous laid eyes on this picture, Pope Kyrillos would appear to him in his full appearance. This matter was repeated many times, as well as other apparitions.

His claivrance:

"The Spirit of God came upon him...The utterance of him who hears the words of God, Who sees the vision of the Almighty, Who falls down, with eyes wide open." (Numbers 24: 2-4)

Introduction:

We spoke in the previous section about the relationship that Fr Mettaous enjoyed with Heaven and the heavenlies, first of whom was St Mary.

We now explore his knowledge of the future, however in little detail as we are unable to expand on this topic for its vast details and frequent occurrences. We will explore how he was able to see, despite not being able to see physically. He could describe materialistic things with such accuracy and detail as if he were seeing them physically! His knowledge of secret matters also astounded many, especially his knowledge of things that happened in the past! His knowledge of the future also became apparent, especially about matters occurring in places far away from him!

We mentioned earlier that Fr Mettaous lost his sight in 1987, but did anybody doubt that he could see just like a person with sight would see?! Would anybody dare act in the presence of Fr Mettaous as if he were not able to see them? The answer is definitely not!

His eminent honour, high spiritual level and his apparent sainthood did not allow anybody to think even that Fr Mettaous had a physical disability, i.e. his loss of sight. If this happened, it would happen much later on in the relationship with him and sometimes only when he revealed it to them! They would not believe it because they saw Fr Mettaous acting as if he actually saw, very much like them! For he sometimes pointed at things and people as if he could really see them!

Fr Mettaous affected many people with this talent and many can vouch for such a gift; whether it be from monks in the same monastery, sons in confession or laymen such as his doctors and nurses.

the same day, the father of the child had booked a ticket for his son to return to Egypt to his mother.

Fr Mettaous's words became true to the letter! The mother was surprised to open the door of her apartment on the same day to see her son knocking. She could not withhold herself and so she came to explain to me what God has done for her.

Chapter 6

A Thankful Sick Person

"Blessed is the man who endures temptation; for when he has been approved, he will receive the crown of life which the Lord has promised to those who love Him." (James 1: 12)

It may be true that most of the people knew of Fr Mettaous as a result of his illness, which extended for over a third of a century (from 1976 until his departure in 2008). This is more than half of the time he spent in monasticism, which was close to 60 years (1949 -2008).

However, we all saw in him the thankful sick person that he was. He endured in great silence and great perseverance. The Lord crowned him with many crowns, but the most valuable of all was the crown of enduring sickness and pain with amazing thanksgiving, with which he ended his acceptable and valid perseverance.

He might have repeated the words, "if indeed we suffer with Him, that we may also be glorified together. For I consider that the sufferings of this present time are not worthy to be compared with the glory which shall be revealed in us." (Rom 8: 17-18)

There is a story mentioned in the Paradise of Desert Fathers, which puts into perspective the high standing of Fr Mettaous in Heaven, amid the Lord and the Heavenly saints and martyrs.

One of the elders said that he saw four ranks in Heaven:

The first: A sick person who endures, thanking God

The second: A well person who invites the strangers and consoles the weak

The third: A person who is struggling in solitude of the desert

The fourth: A disciple who obeys his master for the sake of God

Let us, dear reader, delve into this flowering paradise and smell the sweet aroma of Christ, along with the scent of the virtues of Fr Mettaous.

The beginning of the sickness from 1976 till 1987:

"I will bring the one-third through the fire, Will refine them as silver is refined, and test them as gold is tested. They will call on My name, And I will answer them. I will say, `This is My people'; And each one will say, `The Lord is my God.'" (Zech 13: 9)

In 1976, Fr Mettaous found out that he was diabetic and had high blood pressure. Later that year, he was also diagnosed with glaucoma – an increase in ocular pressure, with the accompanying pain in the eyes.

This was the beginning of the journey of treatment and sicknesses, along with its pains and struggles. He was introduced to hospitals and surgery theatres. He received seven eye surgeries between 1976 and 1987, with the first surgery done on 19th of July 1976.

We found this powerful sentence written by Fr Mettaous and dated 06/05/1957, which is thirty years before he had lost his sight.

"If I determine to be in the light; then be blessed, if I determined to be in darkness; then be blessed, also! If you wanted to console me, then be blessed, and if you determined to afflict me with more sorrows, then be blessed forever."

Fr Mettaous El Suriany

How do we interpret it?!

Was this his inner sense that he will, one day, venture through the path of pain and tribulation? In like manner did Balaam prophesy saying, "I see Him, but not now; I behold Him, but not near" (Numbers 24: 17)

However, he did show a willingness to accept temptation and to carry the cross, which the Lord had appointed for him, with complete thanksgiving.

Or did God inform him, as He did with the father of all fathers, Abraham, when He wanted to demolish the cities of Sodom and Gomorrah, "Shall I hide from Abraham what I am doing" (Gen 18: 17). However, he accepted and obeyed, saying with David the Psalmist, "Whom have I in heaven but You? And there is none upon earth that I desire besides You." (Ps 73: 25)

We do not know, and nobody has the answer!

We witnessed and knew that Fr Mettaous was a strong and clear example of a person who is tempted and was accepting tribulation with all joy and thanksgiving.

We now resume our recount of Fr Mettaous's tribulation with the cross of suffering and the details of how he lost his sight.

We mentioned earlier that Fr Mettaous had a few eye diseases and he received treatment for more than ten years until he was diagnosed with Cataracts.

Normally, a person diagnosed with cataracts would receive appropriate surgical treatment, but due to Fr Mettaous's history of eye diseases, he was in great danger if he did receive surgery. However, according to Fr Mettaous's personal wishes and through the guidance of a well known eye surgeon, Dr Mamdouh Fakhry

Bakhoum, he accepted the treatment through surgery and may the will of the Lord be done.

The surgery was done and what has happened, did happen... It was God's choice that Fr Mettaous ceased to see! However, his physical sight stopped so that his inner eyes could be opened to spiritual visions and heavenly revelations.

When Dr Mamdouh Fakhry Bakhoum learnt of the surgery's outcome, he feared   Fr Mettaous' reaction when he found out. However, to his amazement and shock, Fr Mettaous said calmly and with a steady voice, "Are you upset? I had retinal detachment for ten years and should have lost my sight years ago, but the Lord granted me ten years extra to see and I thank God for this. And after all, God took away my sight, but has given me foresight."

Truly wondrous is this amazing and complete surrender to God's will. Is this the natural reaction of someone who has just lost his sight? However, it is his complete and utter surrender to God's Holy will, "and the peace of God, which surpasses all understanding" (Phil 4: 7) which filled his whole being.

This brings us to the saying of the great St Anthony, the Father of monks, to St Didimous the Blind, who had lost his sight at the age of four and who later become the Chancellor of the   Theological College in Alexandria in the fourth century.   St Anthony said to him, "Do not be disheartened, my friend Didimous, that you lost the sight that we share with insects and animals, but rather rejoice that God has granted you the inner eyes, which you share with the heavenly angels, in seeing the Glory of God. It is this foresight that enabled you to comprehend God and see His light shining in the darkness of your eyes, so that your heart is enlightened."

History tells us that these simple, yet very deep and powerful words were a great condolence to the blind St Didimous for the rest of his life.

What is worth mentioning here is that after he had lost his sight for a long time, I asked him what he would do if medical progress enabled him to treat his condition in the future. He replied instantaneously and simply, "My father, this matter is gone and is behind my back for a very long time now! I thank God for everything; in the light, I am with Him, and in darkness, I am also with Him."

His main goal was to be with God in continual companionship in the light of the body, or in darkness. The two matters were equal to him.

The first few years in darkness:

"He has aged my flesh and my skin, And broken my bones. He has besieged me And surrounded me with bitterness and woe." (Lamentations 3: 4-5)

After his painful struggle with losing his sight, Fr Mettaous settled down medically, despite the minor problems that accompanied his diabetes and high blood pressure.

His health status was maintained for a while, until the end of 1996, when he suffered a stroke in the right side of his brain, which led to complete paralysis to his left side (i.e., his left hand and leg). This forced him down to the El Hayaa hospital to receive appropriate treatment. He was detained for twenty-six days to monitor his health status by specialist doctors.

This extended stay forced him to have a permanent catheterisation, which remained with him for nearly twelve years! Many would know the major complications and the utter pain that accompany catheterisation for such a long period.

The year of strokes 1998:

"The whole head is sick, and the whole heart faints." (Isa 1: 5)

In the beginning of 1998, Fr Mettaous suffered restriction to his coronary artery, as well as two strokes in his heart, heart failure and pulmonary oedema, as well as other medical issues, which we shall recount in a later part.

On Thursday 25/6/1998, Fr Mettaous suffered another stroke in his brain, which led to deterioration of his health. Due to his illness, he was forced to stay in the hospital for 85 days consecutively – spending most of his time in checkups, pathology tests and physiotherapy to improve the outcome of his stroke.   However, there was no sign of improvement to his left side, which had been paralysed.

Since this complication, he has been bedridden due to his left-side paralysis and he would rarely get up, except to go to the toilet and use a wheelchair.

Eleven years prior to his stroke, he had been lost his sight, as we mentioned earlier.

While the flesh was bound to these two very significant and traumatic incidents, both physically and emotionally, his strong spirit flew above the realm of the flesh and its weakness.

I recall in his last days, Fr Mettaous suffered from acute blockage to the circulation of his lower extremities.   He faced the possibility of amputation. I said to Fr Mettaous, "Father, make the sign of the Cross on your legs because the doctors say that there is a chance they will have to amputate them." He was very calm and collected when he responded, "No problem, all of this is going to dust!"

Since that time, Fr Mettaous was known to be bedridden, paraplegic, with a permanent catheter attached to his body and living in darkness, according to medical terms. This is the state:

"He has no form or comeliness; And when we see Him, There is no beauty that we should desire Him." (Isa 53: 2)

Despite these painful circumstances, yet his face shone with amazing joy and peace and it was this fact that was a source of comfort to those who were in pain and tempted.

He was astounding in his silence, for he was more of a living sermon than of a speaker. If he ever spoke, and he had few words to say, then "His mouth is most sweet, yes, he is altogether lovely." (Songs 5: 16)

His face was joyful and calm, shining peace and holiness to others around him. Many say what St. Joseph said to the great St Anthony, "It is enough to just behold your face, father."

Just being in his presence was a source of awe, reverence and admonishment. If the "bodily presence is weak" (2 Cor 10: 10), yet his presence had a deep and moving impact on a lot of people.

A broken left foot (May, 2005):

"From the sole of the foot even to the head, There is no soundness in it, But wounds and bruises and putrefying sores; They have not been closed or bound up, Or soothed with ointment." (Isa 1: 6)

On Friday 27/5/2005, while Fr Mettaous was attempting to go to the bathroom, he fell and broke his left foot (the same foot that was paralysed). He was transported to the hospital for medical examination and for a routine x-ray to be taken. It was discovered that he had a broken ankle. The medical supervisors started to negotiate treatment options for Fr Mettaous, in order to treat the broken ankle.

Should the ankle be put in a cast? Should they surgically intervene to place metal screws and a metal plate? Due to the fact that the left leg had a lot of skin boils – due to the poor blood circulation to the foot – the idea of the cast was dismissed, since the cast could worsen the boils, which could lead to gangrene in the whole foot.

All thoughts were redirected towards surgical intervention, and so another x-ray was taken to identify the blood supply to the foot. However, the scan showed shortage in blood supply, which meant that surgical intervention could not be chosen – since the wound would not be able to heal properly due to the poor blood circulation.

The doctors settled for the second best choice of using a plaster cast, but due to constant friction with the skin, new skin ulcers developed, the pain became unbearable and no pain killers worked.

From the excessive pain, Fr Mettaous lapsed into a coma, which lasted for three weeks, while he passed through excruciating pain. He only knew one sentence, "Thank you Lord", which he did not stop repeating.

Finally, the doctors decided to put the leg in a cast, while opening windows in the cast where the ulcers had developed, so that they could heal faster. And the procedure went forth; they put the broken bones back into their natural position and put the foot in a cast. All of these procedures took place without using local or general anaesthesia! He stayed in the hospital for a further two weeks, after which he returned to the monastery. His foot remained in the cast for two months, but, unfortunately, the broken bone did not heal. As it is written in the Bible "He bruises, but He binds up", for after they took off the cast, all the skin ulcers that developed on his foot had completely healed.

Fr Mettaous lived for three years until his departure with the broken bone not completely healed. After these three years, he departed in peace. He reminds us of what St Paul said, "For I bear in my body the marks of the Lord Jesus" (Gal 6: 17).

Many times I would only find out that Fr Mettaous was in pain if I asked him, yet he never complained. I would, on occasion, cry out of compassion for Fr Mettaous's health status. He would say to me, "Why are you crying now? I am the man who should be upset, but I am thankful towards God for everything." I would say to him, "Why did God allow this, then? Isn't it enough that your leg is paralysed, now it's broken too?!" He would respond in a very calm, even angelic, manner and say, "Do you want me to say to you what Job said to his wife, 'You speak as one of the foolish women speaks. Shall we indeed accept good from God, and shall we not accept adversity?' (Job 2: 10) I thank God for everything." I would be so embarrassed by his answer and his complete submission to God's will and his endurance throughout all his physical agony.

On this note

We remember a nice comment, or rather a deep contemplation, by Dr Ayman Henein, who was one of the doctors supervising Fr Mettaous after he broke his foot. When the wound would not heal, Fr Mettaous was unable to step with it on the ground, he said, "God did not allow Fr Mettaous to set his foot on the ground because the ground is unworthy of his footstep!"

The truly marvellous thing to happen to Fr Mettaous was that, despite being bedridden for the last twelve years of his life, he never developed bed sores, which is a true miracle by all means.

If we look at his past medical history, we find out that Fr Mettaous went to the El Hayaa hospital approximately 30 times in his last twelve years and was hospitalised for nearly 450 days. He entered the surgical theatre more than 15 times, and was on so many medications that he used to take about 30 tablets and five injections daily. This was normal in a regular situation, but during medical emergencies, the number of tablets used to double sometimes.

Along with the list provided, he also suffered from dental issues, which made eating and chewing a very painful process. The only way to feed Fr Mettaous was by processing his food into a liquid form, which made the food have no taste or texture.

There was not one organ in his body that was not affected by some sort of disease, but the grace of God worked greatly in his damaged body.

"As unknown, and yet well known; as dying, and behold we live; as chastened, and yet not killed; as sorrowful, yet always rejoicing; as poor, yet making many rich; as having nothing, and yet possessing all things." (2 Cor 6: 9-10)

The spiritual contemplation of Fr Mettaous regarding enduring his physical temptation of sickness

"Bringing every thought into captivity to the obedience of Christ." (2 Cor 10: 5)

We saw in this chapter how Fr Mettaous persevered through the tribulations of great sickness and various illnesses. He carried his Cross of pain for more than thirty years, i.e. more than half of the time he spent as a monk and more than a third of his life here on earth. He endured the Cross of pain with thanksgiving, joy, perseverance and endurance that exceeds the threshold of human beings. He never once complained about his pain, but he never even prayed to God to be healed. When I asked him before, "Father, pray to the Lord to heal you," and he replied, "How can I ask Him to heal me, when He allowed the sickness in the first place?!" It is such a way of thinking that cannot be fathomed, and is so simple yet deep and meaningful.

I remember one day I asked Fr Mettaous, "Ask the Lord Jesus Christ to heal you," and he answered and said to me, "He can see and knows without me asking Him." I said to him, "Even the great St Paul asked to be healed from the thorn of his flesh once, twice, and even three times!" He laughed at me and replied, "And what happened after St Paul asked to be healed once, twice and three times? The Lord said to him 'My grace is sufficient for you, for My strength is made perfect in weakness...The Lord allowed for sickness, then how can I ask Him to take it away?!"

I used to remain quiet, unable to contradict him or answer him, but I used to muse at his spiritual philosophy and this amazing spiritual thought regarding enduring the Cross of pain with thanksgiving and joy, "He who is able to accept it, let him accept it." (Matt 19: 12)

Chapter 7

His Departure

Fear and humility raise the head of a celibate and when he departs, he illuminates with them.

St. Efraim the Syrain

My Lord, when will I depart? How? Where to? All these questions are hidden with You. But regarding my departure, there is no doubt that I will journey to You, the Loving Lord. I know that through my own works, I shall not sustain salvation, but I have Your Love and Your Precious Blood, along with the unshakable faith that all the powers of darkness cannot hinder my soul when it leaves my body to meet with You.

From here begins my victory with the One whom I love for I must rise and be with Him. When I take off this perishing body, when it lays in dust, I shall start a new life. Therefore, death is not the end, but rather a beginning; when should my departure be?

Farewell, my earthly body, for I shall reunite with you in a much more beautiful and glorified image. Farewell, the one who enjoyed my companionship among them, for we shall meet with the Beloved in Glory – farewell, O places that clothed my body. I am going to a better and everlasting place. Farewell, O natures with all its condoling imageries, for you have consoled me here on earth.

Fr. Mettaous El Suriany

These powerful and deep words were written by Fr Mettaous on 11/6/1957 before his departure by about 51 years. He affixed in front of him this hour – the hour of departure from his body, from the beginning of his monastic life and all the way to the end. He neared 60 years of struggle towards this moment.

When he wrote these words, he had already spent about eight years in monasticism and was in the late thirties – so he was in the prime of his life. He had his eyes set upon what St Isaac the Syrian said, "I have been waiting all my life for this moment!"

Fr Mettaous passed through many health complications, that could have easily ended his life, without much misery or pain, but "His hour had not yet come." (John 7: 30)

The beginning of the end:

"The day began to wear away." (Luke 9: 12)

On Tuesday of Jonah's fast, 19/2/2008, after the completion of the Holy Liturgy, Bishop Mettaous the Abbot of the Monastery came to visit Fr Mettaous in his cell, to ask about his health and to direct to him an invitation to attend the prayers of the consecration of the new church in the monastery, which was going to be consecrated by Pope Shenouda III on Saturday 23/2/2008. Bishop Mettaous asked Fr Mettaous to attend the prayers of consecrations, but Fr Mettaous replied and said, "Believe me, Father, I do not know how my health will be on that day!"

Indeed it happened, on Thursday morning of Jonah's Feast, 21/2/2008, his health started to deteriorate fast, so he was transported back to the hospital for further tests. By sunset of the same day, pathology results came out with the following results:

Firstly:
Deteriorated kidney function and a detrimental increase in urea and creatinine levels.

Secondly:
A great decrease in the clotting ability of the blood (INR 5.9, instead of the normal 1)

Thirdly:

90% blockage in the arteries providing blood to the feet, from the knee to the foot, which meant there was a big chance the doctors would have to amputate the legs above the knees.

The supervising doctors began to work on improving the kidney function, so that they could insert a stent to widen the arteries of the legs. This procedure is known to involve injecting a dye, which was not appropriate at that stage, due to the deteriorating kidney function.

I remember, after spending a few days in hospital with Fr Mettaous, that I said to him, "Get well soon, Father, we want to return to the monastery before the beginning of Lent." He answered me, "No...This time it will take longer in hospital!"

After ten days of staying in the hospital, Fr Mettaous began to get worse. His countenance was very pale and dry, as he was taking a lot of diuretic medications to get rid of excess fluid and to help with his kidney failure. He was on 96cm of Lasix (48 injections of Frusemide). He was on a medication to bring down his temperature, which was consistently high, as well as very potent antibiotics. This was accompanied by the normal amount of medications, which he used to take on a regular basis; 30 tablets a day.

On the Sunday before Lent, a group of monks were visiting Fr Mettaous and at the end of the visit a monk said to him, "Fr Mettaous, we are heading back to the monastery, are you coming with us?" He replied, with such effort and pain on his face, "This is it...the body is tired...I am going home."

After a few days of this last visit, Fr Mettaous was in deep sleep, when suddenly he opened his eyes and stared at the ceiling, while shouting, "Absolve me fathers, absolve me fathers."

I realised what was happening, and so I asked Fr Mettaous, "Where are these fathers? There is nobody in the room except for us." He nodded at the ceiling and said, "There they are, can't you see them?" I said to him, "Honestly, I cannot see anyone! Who are these fathers?" He replied with a sad countenance, "They are the fathers that brought me to monasticism...there they are...and I am asking them to absolve me!"

Inserting a Centreline:

Fr Mettaous's kidney function steadily decreased, and the urine output was decreasing, which resulted in a higher level of urea and creatinine in the blood. The supervising doctors decided to insert a Centreline from the neck, which detects the blood levels of certain blood works (CVP), which showed that the level of these blood works were many times the usual normal level.

Severe haemorrhage into the stomach:

On Wednesday 19/3/2008 on the Feast of the Cross, Fr Mettaous suffered from severe hypotension (reduction in blood pressure) and so the doctors started treating Fr Mettaous for the hypotension by injecting him with specific medications. However, the blood pressure did not respond but continued dropping.

At 2am of Thursday 20/3/2008, Fr Mettaous was moved to the CCU (Continuous Care Unit), and once he was there, his heart stopped. The doctors started reviving the heart, by injecting him with Adrenaline to start the heart. God was glorified again and Fr Mettaous's heart started beating once more. In the morning, a tube was inserted from the nose to the stomach (Rail). The doctors discovered that there was a severe haemorrhage in the stomach and so they started to clean the stomach; a process that took about

2 hours. As a consequence of this sudden haemorrhage, there was a severe depletion in haemoglobin in his blood and so he was set up for a blood transfusion. He received more than ten bags of blood, as well as nine bags of plasma.

However, the haemorrhage did not stop, and so they performed an endoscopy (a small camera that goes down to the stomach) to try and inject the bleeding vessels. However, the stomach wall was bleeding heavily and so we left the matter in God's hands.

A stroke in the brain stem that caused complete paralysis:

Finally, the haemorrhage was under control on Saturday 22/3/2008, and so he was taken out of the intensive care room. After three days, however, we realised that Fr Mettaous could not move his right hand or leg and there was a dramatic increase in blood ammonia level , a severe deterioration in kidney function and a deterioration in the efficacy of the heart. Fr Mettaous was having a lot of trouble trying to breathe.

The doctors performed two CT scans to find out what was happening, but nothing showed up. Finally, they performed an MRI scan, which also showed nothing. Two days later, they performed the MRI again, which showed a stroke in the brain stem.

Fr Mettaous's health began to deteriorate generally; complete paralysis, chronic kidney failure, inability to speak, and a systematic shutdown. It was as if God were preparing us for what was about to happen. This reminds us of King Hezekiah, when the Lord sent him Isaiah with a message saying, "Thus says the Lord: `Set your house in order, for you shall die, and not live.'" (2 Kings 20: 1)

Inserting a tube into the stomach:

During the time that he spent in the CCU, he received nutrients through a stomach tube and the rail that was inserted through his nose.

However, after the stroke that led to complete paralysis, the doctors started to think of alternative methods to feed Fr Mettaous, due to the problems that developed through the use of the rail. They decided to insert a tube into his stomach to feed him.

It is known that such a procedure is very simple, they apply a local anaesthetic, make a small incision in the stomach wall and affix the tube in a certain manner – a procedure that takes no longer than 10 minutes. Indeed, the procedure was done successfully, but nobody suspected the results.

The surgeons discovered a severe haemorrhage in the liver, and they immediately started a large incision in the stomach wall, which measured 15 cm, in an effort to find out the reason behind the haemorrhage. After two hours of intensive work, the surgeons finally put a stop to the bleeding and so by the end of the procedure, Fr Mettaous ended up with a large 15 cm cut to his stomach wall, as well as the stomach tube. The doctors set him up for a blood transfusion to replace the lost blood.

During these tough times and the unbearable pain, he must have experienced, Fr Mettaous's face was shining with peace and comfort that mesmerised all who saw him.

Complete kidney shutdown:

The urine output declined gradually, until Sunday 30/3/2008, when the kidneys finally completely shut down. We waited for God to work this time, but, unfortunately, his status declined. He had oedema in all parts of his body, which made him look inflated. There was no other way but to start dialysis.

On Thursday 3/4/2008, the supervising doctors decided that dialysis was crucial now and so they transported Fr Mettaous to El Salam Hospital in El-Mohandeseen since there was no dialysis unit available in the El Hayaa Hospital.

On the same night, the secretary of Pope Shenouda III called the hospital, informing the hospital that His Holiness would be visiting Fr Mettaous at 6 pm.

At 6:30 pm, His Holiness was in Fr Mettaous's room and was exceedingly moved with compassion towards his health status. He prayed over him the Absolution Prayer and asked him about his latest health updates. He became more upset when he found out the details. He commented saying, "It is a waste...It is a waste, last time I saw Fr Mettaous he was much better than now. What happened to him? He was the confession father to most of the monks in the monastery, may the Lord heal him and be with you all." He left and was very upset about Fr Mettaous's health.

After His Holiness had left, Fr Mettaous was transported by an ambulance to El Salam Hospital to undertake the dialysis procedure. He was prepared for dialysis at 8 pm.

At 1:30 am of Friday morning 4/4/2008, he was prepared for another cycle of dialysis, when suddenly his blood pressure dropped to 70/30 and this time Fr Mettaous was so close to passing away. The dialysis machine was switched off at once and Fr Mettaous was taken off it; unfortunately even dialysis was no longer a valid option. At 4 am, Fr Mettaous was back in his room in El Hayaa Hospital once again.

His return to El Surian Monastery:

"Let us return to the monastery, for a sign of the salvation of a monk is his departure inside his monastery."

Pope Gabriel the Seventh, the 95th Patriach

After Fr Mettaous had returned to El Hayaa Hospital, his status was going from bad to worse. On Sunday morning 6/4/2008, his body was so inflated because his body could not get rid of excess fluids, which had reached the top of his lungs. We would perform suction from his lungs to aid in his breathing.

At 3 pm of the same day, the supervising doctors came into his room and admitted their complete and regrettable inability to perform any more procedures to improve Fr Mettaous's health status. Based on this information, I called Bishop Mettaous, the Abbot of the Monastery, and explained to him the situation. He decided that Fr Mettaous should return to the monastery.

Even if God determined to take Fr Mettaous up to heaven, at least he should be in his monastery, between his beloved children.

And indeed, the ambulance was prepared to take Fr Mettaous back to the monastery.

On the evening of Sunday 6/4/2008, Fr Mettaous left the hospital for the last time, amid all the tears of those around him, finally farewelling him. These tears were the biggest proof of how much all these people loved Fr Mettaous. They felt deep inside that they would not see Fr Mettaous again. They would no longer see this heavenly visitor walking among them, or emerge in his bountiful joy, humility, calmness and peace.

Despite being unable to speak, he would have said, "I go the way of all the earth, do not weep for Me, but weep for yourselves and for your children." (1 Kings 2: 2, Luke 23: 28)

His arrival at the monastery

Did you know, dear reader, that the distance between the hospital and the monastery is about 200km and that it takes about two to three hours to travel that distance, when taking into consideration the busy traffic in Cairo, and any emergencies that could occur on the way.

But it was God's will that he be transported as quickly as possible and so it took an hour and a half from the hospital to the door of his cell in the monastery. It was God's wisdom to allow Fr Mettaous to remain alive until the monks of the monastery could see his countenance for the last time, to take his blessings and to bid him farewell before his departure.

And indeed, Fr Mettaous arrived at the monastery at 8:30 pm, accompanied by a team of doctors and nurses. Awaiting him were all the fathers and monks of the monastery and the surrounding monasteries. He was taken down from the ambulance, surrounded by more than a hundred monks, and the atmosphere was very majestic and emotional. One monk kisses Fr Mettaous with tears down his face, another prays for his recovery and another thanks God that he got the opportunity to see Fr Mettaous while he was still alive, before his departure to heaven.

The Release of the Spirit:

"For I am already being poured out as a drink offering, and the time of my departure is at hand. I have fought the good fight, I have finished the race, I have kept the faith. Finally, there is laid up for me the crown of righteousness, which the Lord, the righteous Judge, will give to me on that Day." (2 Tim 4: 6-8)

Fr Mettaous was escorted back to the cell that he loved and which he built and watered with his tears and blood. The cell that witnessed his sufferings and excruciating pain and which also witnessed his glory and holiness. It was God's will that his soul did not depart, until he sat again on his throne, I mean his bed of sickness, on which he was crucified for twelve years.

Fr Mettaous spent 45 days in hospital during the last visit and so he was very keen on returning to his cell to bid it a last farewell. All the fathers gathered around him, starting with Bishop Mettaous, the Abbot of the Monastery, who was sitting next to him.

The monks and fathers began to individually prostrate themselves in front of Fr Mettaous, one by one and kiss his pure and holy hands and head. Some of them kissed his feet to receive his blessings and to ask him to pray for them.

It was a very emotional time, and the quietness was very powerful. The only sound that could be heard was the sound of Fr Mettaous gasping for breath.

If you looked around, all you could see were many faces with tears on them and sad countenances and death roaming around the place.

One minute before 10:30 pm that night, Fr Mettaous opened his humble eyes and looked around him in complete peace and tranquillity, as if bidding them all farewell with whatever energy that remained in him.

In utter tranquillity, his spirit was released to heaven, amid the rejoicing of the heavenlies and the tears of the earthlies. This was the moment that Fr Mettaous had longed for and struggled for all these years, until he was united with his Groom and Saviour, the Lord Jesus Christ, who would wipe away all his tears and say to him: "Enough pain, my beloved Mettaous."

His wrist watch stopped at the same moment when his soul departed from his body, to mark the beginning of eternal life with God and His angels and saints.

His enshrouding and transporting to the Church:

Every time Fr Mettaous would go to hospital to receive medical attention, I would pack his white Tunic and Cowl, in the unfortunate event that he might pass away.

This used to happen every time, except for the last time, when I did not pack his white Tunic and Cowl, for I said to myself, "I have been taking this tunic and cowl for ten years now and I always return with it. There is no need for it." It is amazing that this was the first time for ten years that one of the ladies that loved Fr Mettaous brought him a white Tunic and Cowl as a gift when she came to visit him.

I did not know that these were the clothes, which God had prepared to enshroud the pure body of Fr Mettaous.

After all the monks finished taking blessing from Fr Mettaous, all the medical equipment that was attached to Fr Mettaous was taken away, such as the Centreline, stomach tube and the catheter. We note here that we could not take out the stitches that held the stomach wound when the liver was discovered to haemorrhage. It was left behind as a sign and a reminder of the pain and endurance on this land of suffering.

We enshrouded the body of Fr Mettaous with the clothes of priesthood and Bishop Mettaous, the Abbot of the Monastery, insisted on clothing him with his own cloak.

The procession of taking his holy body to the church began at

11 pm that night. It was the first time that he was carried out of his cell, knowing that he would not return to it again. He was carried on shoulders, just as he carried everybody in his heart. He was carried amid the joyous tunes and singing of the monks.

They walked around the church carrying his body and finally placed him in front of the door of the altar. The monks and fathers began to pray the entire book of Psalms, followed by the book of Revelations, until the bell sounded for Midnight Praises (Tasbeha). The Praises were followed by Raising of Morning Incense and the Holy Liturgy, which concluded at 8:30 am the next morning. The funeral prayers were set to start at 10 am. The fathers and monks decided to read the book of John until it was 10 o'clock.

They stopped at chapter 17 of the book of John, where Christ was interceding for His disciples during the last meeting between Christ and His holy disciples. They stopped at this verse: "Father, I desire that they also whom You gave Me may be with Me where I am, that they may behold My glory which You have given Me; for You loved Me before the foundation of the world." (John 17: 24)

At ten o'clock, a multitude of monks, priests and bishops from other monasteries entered the church and the prayers commenced on the body of Fr Mettaous, amid the tears of many who stood around him. The prayers were in the joyous tune, commemorating the Feast of the Annunciation as if heaven were rejoicing by receiving her son from our world.

After the prayers, the body was carried in another procession around the altar and then around the church. Everyone was so keen to carry his body, out of their love for him and to farewell him.

He was carried to the new Tafoos, exactly like his Lord, who was buried in a new tomb, which nobody has used before (John 19:

41). This happened at midday. This concluded almost three hours of praying over his body.

We went back to our own cells, crying the loss of the fatherhood, the gentleness, the caring, the attention and the love of our beloved father; crying for him to remember us and to intercede for us so that we may complete our struggle, just as he did. Thus, we would stand around, and he would say: "Here am I and the children whom God has given Me." (Heb 2: 13)

Chapter 8

His Letters

Between your hands, Dear Reader, lie some of Fr Mettaous's letters, which he addressed to some of his beloved fathers and brethren, among whom are also some bishops. These are not just normal letters, but when you read them, you begin to fathom the depth and spiritual clarity of his sweet words. You will discover that each letter is a small sermon, and its words are beneficial to all who read it, as it provides guidance and advice in a few lines.

A letter addressed to Bishop Shenouda, the Bishop of Education (who later became Pope Shenouda III)

El Surian Monastery on 9/1/1971

After kissing your holy hands, May you remain blessed and in full health, with increasing fruits of the Holy Spirit, who lives and works in you and others.

This might be the first time I write to one of the bishops who went out of our blessed monastery. I am writing to congratulate you on the Blessed Feast, and to express my love towards your Grace. It is honest love that stems up from the heart, and I am affected because you were not present with us for the first time on a Feast! We were so accustomed to seeing your Grace between us in the monastery, and in the monastic life which we shared.

As for me, the weak and abject man, I long to hear of your presence so I can be sure of your good health.

In conclusion, I kiss your holy and blessed hands, asking for your prayers for me, and hope that you would take the next opportunity to visit the monastery, as it has been so long since you came, and we cannot forget you.

Absolve me, my father, and remember me in your prayers

The Monk Fr Mettaous El Suriany

Some advice and spiritual guidance, which was written by Fr Mettaous to one of his spiritual sons:

El Surian Monastery on 1/8/1975

- I see that people who quote spiritual elders, without the guidance of their confession father, can pose a struggle for others if they start to measure up to them. This is left in the hands of the confession father, who is able to measure up each person according to their individual spiritual level, and their preparedness and endurance.

- Do not quote yourself in writing, so that others may read it.

- Strict awareness in the matter of sitting in the cell, and also the matter of staying up at night, and fasting. It is enough what we have witnessed in this age, which is a matter that needs a lot of love and humility, patience and endurance and a focused goal and a direct target.

- The spiritual guidance provided to a monk should not be told to others, and if need be, it should be in very limited details, and only for the spiritual benefit of others of the monastic race.

- In general, the matter pertaining to your writing may be of benefit to a few, but might be harmful to many.

Fr Mettaous El Suriany

A letter addressed to Monk Shenouda El Antony, regarding his new consecration as a monk:

(who later became Bishop Yustus, the Abbot of the monastery of St Anthony)

My dear and beloved father,

Grace and peace be to you,

Bishop Mettaous was in my presence, and he told me of your monasticism, so I rejoiced and decided to write a letter to congratulate you. Congratulations on carrying the Cross of our Lord and your struggle in the path of your saintly monks and fathers.

What added to my joy was the presence of Bishop Mettaous in the ceremony of your monasticism, by chance, as if God is revealing our love to you. He also put on your monastic garments with his own hands, as a sign of passing down the spirit of monasticism from your beloved brethren, which has been passed down for many generations.

I have great confidence in you that you will be a great monk, living by the light of the Holy Bible and the teachings of the elderly fathers, which are written in the Paradise of Desert Fathers and other books. When you were present with us in the El Surian Monastery, you told us about your great joy and the consecration of your whole life to Christ, from a very young age. And now, the Lord has called for you to live and worship Him in the dwelling of the righteous, away from the world and its lustful desires. Conduct yourself in love and humility, in self-denial and death to the world. In the path of your struggle to Heaven, you will be faced with many obstacles and various trials and wars, for many snares are set up by the devil for every monk, to block his path and push him away from virtues. Humility will ruin every snare, and you will be victorious by the strength of the Lord.

I hope to hear all good news about you, and about your spiritual progress. It is enough to know that we have a father, a brother and a beloved dear friend in the monastery of St Anthony. Bishop Mettaous promised me that, once the siege around the monastery is broken, we will come and visit you – God willing – for I long to take the blessing of the monastery of St Anthony and the holy monks.

My greetings to you and all the fathers and monks, congratulations for your monasticism.

Please remember me always in your prayers

The Monk Fr Mettaous El Suriany

A letter addressed to one of the monks:

(some books were given to Fr Mettaous as a gift)

El Surian Monastery on 1/12/1972

I received your gift with thanksgiving and appreciation, and I smelt from it a sweet aroma that ascended up to Heaven, acceptable before God, for it is the fruit of your effort in researching historic books from the vast history of our great early fathers and monks. Divine grace allowed us to be their spiritual children (for we are all monks). It is a great honour and a crown granted to us from heaven, to be called the sons of the desert of Sheheet (Scetis) and the sons of the Great St Macarious. This is more valuable to us than anything in the world; even more than crowns of kings.

I plead to God, through your prayers, to complete our struggle and to allow us to walk in the same path that our early fathers walked in, and to give us the same spirit of St Macarious. May the Lord bless you, dear brother, for your efforts, and you shall receive comfort in the Heavenly Jerusalem for your efforts, and the work that you have produced for us. You have uncovered a great treasure, and have set a lighthouse to shine light to bring the lost souls, and to shine the grace of God on their hearts, to reject the world and its desires, and come to the desert carrying the cross of their Master, following in the footsteps of His saints.

How joyous is the day when we see our monasteries and deserts filled with monks and strugglers, worshippers of God in Spirit and truth. May God bless you and your spiritual children, who also carry their cross, and may He make them all as shining lights in the Church of our Glorious God.

My greetings and many thanks to your excellence and I ask you to remember me in your prayers.

The Monk Fr Mettaous El Suriany

A letter sent to one of his spiritual sons, who was ordained a monk in the monastery of St Bishoy:

El Surian monastery 4/9/1975

I was overjoyed when I found out about your monasticism, hoping that you will be good yeast in the dwelling of our Lord, and the blessings of our forefathers the saints, who lived in this holy desert – and especially the Great St Bishoy – may their blessings dwell on you. I also hope that you will remain a struggler, to take up their spirit and live and walk in their footsteps. Their good conduct has filled the corners of this world with their transcending spirituality, which will encourage you to walk in the same footsteps which they drew for us. We have taken their place, unworthily to be called their sons or even relatives! Be zealous over the holy monastic path, clothed with humility and self-denial, so that you may be worthy of their intercession and spiritual gifts. And last, but not least, you shall be found fit to inherit with them in the Heavenly Jerusalem.

Congratulations on carrying the Cross of your Lord, remember me in your prayers.

May the Lord assist you with His strength, and fill you with His grace, glory be to Him forever.

The Monk Fr Mettaous El Suriany

A letter addressed to one of his friends, who was ordained a monk in one of the monasteries:

El Surian Monastery 7/9/1973

I heard that you have taken a step forward in the struggle of this world – a step that will change the whole path of your life, so I was overjoyed. For what profit is it to a man if he gains the whole world and loses his soul? I, therefore, congratulate you on carrying the Cross of your Master, the Cross that will lead us to the Heavenly Glory. St Macarious the great carried his cross, and his children after him took up their cross.

Therefore, be faithful in the calling which you have been honoured with, to be called a faithful son in the desert of Sheheet (Scetis), so that you may be granted to inherit their eternal inheritance. May the Lord guard you from all evil and work of the devil, and the snares that shall be set against you in the pathway to Heaven. It shall be a blessing that you would bring back the past monastic life, with its glory and splendour. Monasticism is dying to the world, contemplative worshipping, struggling through pain under the feet of the Lord and Master Jesus Christ, being fed by His teachings, and always praising God, growing in His grace and love. This is monasticism that does not pride or knows to be arrogant, and this is the sign of its success.

Do not forget to mention your abject and weak servant in your prayers, who used to pride in your friendship, always asking about your health, and always hoping all the best and peace in your life.

Remain blessed and always growing in the grace of our Lord and the blessings of His saints. Congratulations to you, my friend. Peace to you and best regards to all your fellow brethren in monasticism.

The Lord be with you.

Your brother in Christ, the Monk Fr Mettaous El Suriany

A letter addressed to a father who is struggling in a certain temptation:

El Surian Monastery 22/9/1973

The blessed Hegumen ...

A spiritual kiss and a greeting from the heart, wishing you peace and prosperity. I heard what has happened to you, father – despite the lack of details – however I feel that you are passing through temptation, and I was emotionally moved. I was affected not because of physical matters, since we will leave everything behind, whether we like it or not, but rather I fear that this might have an impact on your temper. God has called us, dear father, for the life of detachment, where we live on this earth as foreigners. Therefore, this is not our true home, but we seek what is everlasting and eternal.

This tribulation, even though it might seem harsh in its essence, is rather a symbol of God's love towards you. For God wants our hearts to be attached to Him alone. Everything here is passing and momentary, but Heaven is eternal and everlasting.

But who am I to impart such knowledge on you, dear father, for you are a father, a teacher and a scholar. However, I wanted to express my spiritual love towards you, and to ensure your peace and emotional and physical stability. I hope for this at all times. May the Lord protect you from all evil and tribulations, and to replace your physical loss with many times over spiritual return, and a Heavenly wage in the Heavenly Jerusalem.

Remain blessed, and remember me in your prayers.

The Monk Fr Mettaous El Suriany

A letter addressed to one of his spiritual children overseas:

El Surian Monastery 17/10/1974

After kissing your holy hands, and wishing you all peace and prosperity and growth in the Spirit and the knowledge of our Lord Jesus Christ, for whom we live, struggle and hopefully attain our goal. I received your letter, which carries your love to me, and I am not worthy of such love. In return, I have nothing to offer but to raise my heart to God in appreciation, praying that He protects you in this new country, with a mighty hand, so that you may be able to love Him and serve Him with an acceptable service. He who allowed you to remain in that place is also able to reap its spiritual fruits, experiences, and helpful tribulations in life. These shall cast a light on your path, to walk in your path in peace and serenity. Knowing that what profit is it to a man if he gains the whole world and loses his own soul.

There is no profit, but to walk with a pure heart, on the light of the Lord's commandments, which facilitates our entry into the Kingdom of Heaven, and to receive the good share. May the Lord make us worthy of such grace, forgiving our sins, through the intercessions of St Mary and all the saints.

I hope that you do not forget me in your prayers, and may the Lord complete your days in the wilderness of this world to please Him, and to live according to His good will. Glory be to God forever.

Peace to you and all the beloved fathers in the Lord.

The Lord be with you.

Your brother in the Lord,

The Monk Fr Mettaous El Suriany

A letter addressed to one of his spiritual children overseas:

El Surian Monastery 11/12/1974

I send you my greetings, love and longing, through the name of our Lord Jesus Christ, hoping that you will be joyous and in good health when my letter reaches you.

My dear brother, may the Lord repay you for your efforts, and may He reward you with everlasting life. May He grant you the forgiveness of your sins, mistakes, and spiritual growth, so that you may be worthy of the eternal inheritance of Heavenly glory, that which is prepared for those who do His works, and who reject the world and its vain glories.

May the Lord bless you always, and make you a reason for the blessing and salvation of all those who know you or deal with you. May the Lord protect you in this world with His pure angels.

Peace to you, father, and to all the other beloved fathers in the Lord. From everybody here, we bless you and pray for you.

Do not forget my weak and abject self in your prayers, and may the Lord complete the days of our wilderness in the flesh according to His own Good Will, and may He assist us for the salvation of our souls. This is our endeavour in this life.

Through the intercessions of St Mary and all the saints, Amen.

Remain blessed.

Your brother,

The Monk Fr Mettaous El Suriany.

Section 2

Sayings From a Contemporary Monk

PREFACE

On 27th September 1999, El Sourian Monastery celebrated the Golden Jubilee of the monasticism of the Reverend Father Mettaous El Souriani. He was a monk for 50 years, spanning a long and fruitful period.

We honour him because he honoured the Lord in his life and monasticism, as He says, "those who honour Me I will honour" (1 Sam 2:30).

We are following St Paul's advice, "Let the elders who rule well be counted worthy of double honor, especially those who labor in the word and doctrine" (1 Tim 5:17). He has toiled, and still does, instructing and teaching his disciple the monks, guiding them toward the path of salvation and eternal life through his words and deeds.

He came to the monastery on 12th May 1949 seeking monasticism and was ordained a monk on 27th September 1949 by the hands of the Abbot of the monastery, the late Bishop Theophilus. He was ordained a priest on 22nd October 1950, and then Hegumen on 7th October 1951. He came to the monastic life at a time when just living in a monastery was a great struggle.

At that time the monastery was a set of ancient ruins in the desert, with no water or plants. The cells were very simple, with straw mats used for sleeping on the floor. It was a very primitive, poor and uncomfortable lifestyle, with very few monks able to lead this very strict monastic life.

There was external comfort of any kind; whoever wanted to stay in the monastery needed to receive his comfort directly from God by remaining in his cell, offering fervent prayers and reading the Holy scriptures and spiritual books; otherwise he would find himself returning to the world, having been unable to bear the hard monastic life in the wilderness.

Fr. Mettaous faced this harsh life and never returned to the world.

He bore everything happily and thankfully, saying: "I would live in the monastery even if it were the furnace of Babylon," referring to the furnace prepared for the three young men (Dan 3:20).

In the early sixties, Pope Shenouda was present in the monastery as Father Antonious El Syriany. He was responsible for duties such as building and planting. He had a strong friendship with Fr. Mettaous that still exists today and helped him to build a separate cell in the monastery garden. This was the first cell to be built outside the monastery's walls. Fr. Antonious personally assisted in its construction, using the very simple equipment available at that time until it was finished and inhabited by Fr. Mettaous, with the Abbot's permission. He still lives there today.

Fr. Mettaous was responsible for duties such as preparing the candles, lanterns and cleaning the church. He would quietly spend the day in his secluded cell, and sleep inside the monastery at night so that he could regularly attend the Midnight Prayers, and then prepare the church for the Holy Liturgy.

Fr. Mettaous is now a revered elder in the monastery. He is greatly loved and honoured by everyone. Until recently, when he was at the height of his health, the monks would gather after the Sunset Prayer to hear a word of benefit concerning the monastic life from him. They would also listen to the biographies of early and contemporary monks, or to the teachings of the early church fathers, as Fr. Mettaous constantly read holy books and scripts, such as St Isaac the Syrian and others. They would then return to their cells filled with a spiritual energy that helped them pursue their monastic struggle.

Fr. Mettaous is a great blessing to the monastery and a source of comfort and spiritual benefit to the monks. He is also a great confession father. Although he doesn't speak as frequently now, just looking at his face and listening to the story of his monastic life and 50 year struggle is sufficient to give a novice monk strength to be patient and remain in his cell without boredom.

Fr. Mettaous likes to read a lot, especially books about the early Church Fathers, the lives of saints and the monastic canons. He even transcribed some of the manuscript of great saints such as the writings of St Isaac and others.

As a result of his continuous reading of the Holy Scripture and spiritual books, he would sometimes write down some personal spiritual contemplations. He has saved these over the past 50 years. On the occasion of the Golden Jubilee of his monasticism, some monks obtained his permission to publish his spiritual contemplations. This book you are reading is one of these publications.

We ask the Lord to prolong the life of Fr. Mettaous, who is a blessing to the monastery and the wilderness, and to grant him good health. We also ask the Lord to make these contemplations a source of blessing to the monks of this generation and to whoever reads them.

Through the intercessions of the Virgin St Mary and the prayers of His Holiness Pope Shenouda III, may the grace of the Lord touch us all.

Bishop Mettaous

Abbot of El Sourian Monastery

The Apostles' Fast 1999

Chapter 1

His Sayings

Holy, Holy, Holy

"The word is very near you, in your mouth and in your heart, that you may do it" (Deut 30:14).

"Do not be afraid, nor be dismayed, for the LORD your God is with you wherever you go" (Joshua 1:5-6;9).

What counts is not how many books you have read or how many sermons you have heard, but your deeds and actions. Wake up, O my soul, for the sunset is approaching and the light around you is fading away, a sign that the end is closer.   14 July 1956

My Lord, when will I leave this world? These are all secrets known only by You. I simply rejoice and am glad when I dream that I am leaving, but when I wake up I grieve when I discover that it was only a dream. As for where I am going, I am sure it is to You, my Beloved kind one. I know that there is no chance of salvation through my deeds, but I trust greatly in Your love and pure Blood. No power on earth can shake me. No hosts of evil can block my soul when it departs this body to meet You, nor can they complain about my sins. If I am a sinner and unworthy, then the Lord Jesus has completed everything and paid my debt. If I could not fast appropriately, the Lord Jesus has fasted on my behalf. If I did not know how to pray, He prayed and kept watch all night on my behalf. Jesus suffered, was buried and arose on my behalf.

My victory comes from Him who loved me, therefore I must rise with Him. When my soul departs my body and my body is buried, I will start a new life, so death is not the end but the beginning. O my Lord, when am I leaving this world? Please fulfil my dreams.

How wonderful is a farewell with the hope of reunion... it is therefore not a farewell, but a hope of meeting again. O my body made of dust I will meet you again in an illuminated, beautiful form.

Farewell those you lived with, you will meet the beloved One there in glory. I am going to the better and everlasting life. Oh nature with all its creation you were a temporary comfort for me, but therein lies eternal comfort. Farewell.

11 June 1957

≫ ✧◦❈◦✧ ≪

The basis of our spiritual and moral growth happens during our youth, when we build our deep roots in piety and virtues. Thus in old age, we reap the fruit of their righteousness.

A soul grows exactly like a tree. The growth of a soul takes place slowly and quietly, as St Isaac said, "If you live in the wilderness, your thoughts will be of the wilderness, and if you mingle with others, you will acquire their thoughts."

The growth of the soul is not limited to life on earth; it keeps growing even in eternity.

22 August 1957

≫ ✧◦❈◦✧ ≪

"Flee sexual immorality" (1 Cor 6: 18)

Our teacher Paul taught us to flee from immorality.

When we battle the pains of immorality, and we feel there are external circumstances that are adding to the strength of this battle, there is no other way out but to escape. Joseph escaped and thus he conquered. If escaping means we leave behind our belongings, or involves being thrown in prison innocently, then the time will come when we are set free by the Truth whom we loved, and purity which we struggled to the point of bloodshed to attain. For we know that our bodies are members of Christ, so how can we make His members immoral members. Therefore, the only option to escape the pain of immorality (after cutting off external influence) is to flee and not to think twice about it.

This is a short method to overcoming the wars of adultery and immorality caused by external circumstances.

7 December 1959

It can be difficult sometimes to let go of the ones whom you love, whom you lived with in this life that is full of worries and sadness. However, if we realise that we are foreigners in this world, and that we await a better life when this body of ours rests in the grave, and that we shall receive inheritence in a building not built with hands, which is everlasting.

The Son asked the Father on our behalf "They are not of the world, just as I am not of the world" (John 17: 16). With great understanding the soul was imprisoned in the flesh, and the first duty of a monk is to free himself from this prison, to release the spirit, even for a little while, to be comforted with the Lord, that the spirit may be fed its spiritual food, just as the body eats to regain its strength, and to fend off the enemies – the hidden and the manifest. This will only happen when the spirit leaves the body indeed.

Feast of Resurrection 1958

Sometimes the strong and clear visitation of grace in many spiritual aspects is noticed by a monk who observes and is aware of the movement of the Spirit within himself.

A wise monk will invest the appropriate time in order to win the precious jewel. During this time, he should control his senses and remain still, no matter what is happening around him. He should depend on the Lord, for this may be the way chosen by the Lord to fulfill his struggle, according to His will.

I have many examples that come to mind, but I can tell you that One Spirit works in many for their salvation and for the welfare of our beloved mother, the One Holy Apostolic Orthodox Church. How wonderful indeed is her teaching, and how sublime the call to monasticism, which is a treasure full of marvelous spiritual teachings. Blessed is he who fulfills its canons accurately, following the teachings of the early fathers St Antonious, St Pakhomius, St Shenouda, St Macarius the Great and many others.

20 July 1958

❧ ❀❀❀ ❦

Sometimes people describe a person as humble or haughty, obedient or disobedient. Why is this, my brethren? Let each one of us consider our own weaknesses. Take out the plank in your own eye first. Do not judge others so that you may not be judged. God forbid that I should talk about people's words or deeds, because we are all facing the One Just Judge.

Here, I would like to warn myself, the miserable weak sinner. May the Lord look upon my humble soul and heal my broken heart.

There is no one who is truly humble except for the Lord Jesus Christ the Incarnate God, who while united with His Father in glory, accepted to humble Himself, giving us what was His and taking what was ours. This is a mystery which surpasses all comprehension.

If someone is described as 'humble,' this is not, in my opinion, a characteristic of human nature, for how can dust be humble? Dust was taken from the ground, so if someone looks at the dust, would he consider it to be pearls or precious stones? Of course not, God forbid! It is therefore justified that when we say, 'humble,' we are simply expressing a description of a person, not a reality, because the only real humility is in the perfect person, the Lord Jesus, the Son of God.

Obedience is also perfected in Jesus; who was obedient to the point of death. Thus we should obey God by fulfilling His commandments as instructed by our saintly fathers.

As for love, which is a degree of perfection, there is no love greater than this: "to lay down his life for his friends," and through it we imitate God "For God so loved the world" (John 15: 13; 3:16).

In my opinion, obedience and humility are intertwined and

united together in love. That is why it is very hard to separate them and describe each on its own.

I personally humble myself and remain faithful to the One I love until death, because "God loves a cheerful giver" (2 Cor 9:7). This is something we do naturally, without any pressure. However as to the feeling of being forced by others to do something good for the sake of love, obedience and humility, I tell you frankly, "No," for the truth taught me we ought to obey God rather than man, and if I am trying to please man I am not yet a servant of Christ.

25 July 1958

There are many traps laid on the spiritual path, and only the humble can escape them. In order for a soul to communicate with its Creator and be united with Him without barriers, it must be purified from the old man. In order to do this, it must pass through many temptations, and then await the work of Grace. What really counts is our humility, our ascetic life and all our other offerings to the Lord so that we may draw His mercy, kindness, benevolence and compassion, yet the hardest and toughest struggles do not pay for the smallest sins. Therefore, we simply have to cling to strong, solid faith in order to be purified by the pure blood which was shed on the cross for the sinners.

26 May 1959

The Lord gave us the parable of the mustard seed that must first fall on the ground and die before it brings forth fruit. We ought not to expect fruits before the tree flourishes. If we expect quick fruits, we will realise that it comes with an expense, in that the tree will wither away quickly.

How can we expect a tree that needs to be fed, and its soil turned, and be watered daily, to bring forth full-grown fruits, if the tree itself is not fully grown yet? I do not know, I wonder sometimes. Does this story negate the parable of the lazy servant who took his talent and buried it? I do understand that this man was given a talent, and he chose to bury it…

May the Lord save my weak self

21 June 1959

Give charitably from what God has given you, and God will increase what He has given you.

This generation spiritualises, but they will never reach true spirituality, because they invent it and create it.

19 June 1970

This generation does not need sermons and lectures; it needs to pass through temptations and tribulations in order to be purified, and then be mentally and spiritually mature enough to live a balanced life.

19 June 1970

How wonderful is the piety resulting from great tribulation and suffering, it is like purified gold. It is not like the piety which has the glittering exterior of sensitivity and politeness in speech and dealings. Herein lies a great danger.

10 October 1970

A monk who is striving for the path of repentance and worship does not spend his day like a hired worker, counting down the hours, but lives as a son living and working for his Father (according to the commandment). Thus he does not feel the boredom of the day or the difficulty of the struggle. This was the life of our early fathers who dwelt in the wilderness. The long years were considered by them as just days in their lives.

3 May 1972

A struggling monk may discover the treasure within himself, for in it is a vital weapon full of comfort and spiritual nourishment that never dries up, aiding in his spiritual growth.

12 July 1972

A real martyr is one who struggles persistently within the realm of his call, not as a pretense or for showing off, but out of a pure heart towards God, rather than towards people. "Let each one remain in the same calling in which he was called" and also "Brethren, let each one remain with God in that state in which he was called" (1 Cor 7:20;24).

3 March 1973

A monk who seeks God seriously and with a pure heart must tolerate injustice, blame, insult, and ridicule. Our Lord Jesus suffered all of this on the Cross, even from His beloved ones. As for those who accept honour, praise, seek leadership, or grumble because of what they are facing, let them know that all their toil is in vain.

23 March 1973

The monastic community which does not have elders who have been struggling in virtues from their youth to their old age is a barren community.

25 March 1973

Great danger comes from mixing worldly teachings with those of the monks living in the wilderness. This means that these monks' lead double lives, as those living in the world have a completely different lifestyle to those living in the wilderness.

25 March 1973

A generation which is weak in virtue, worship and the monastic life will forever live in spiritual weakness. For they love and interact with those who share their sensitivities, shortsightedness and superficial thoughts. This generation avoids the hardships and tribulations of spiritual struggle, living in a fantasy and believing it to be true, but in the end they will feel like they are standing on soft ground and they will sink to the bottom.

12 April 1973

The monk whose lifestyle after becoming a monk is not one hundred times poorer to when he was a layman does not deserve to gain one hundred times the reward for what he has left behind, as promised by the Lord of Glory. This is how the sons of the king (Sts Maximus and Domadius) and the great St Arsanius lived, according to St Paul's words, "I have suffered the loss of all things, and count them as rubbish, that I may gain Christ" (Phil 3:8).

16 April 1973

If the sciences of psychology and philosophy start to permeate the monastic life, they will spoil it completely, just as a weevil does to wood and rust does to metal. Monasticism is based on simplicity, fed by faith, strengthened by hope and confirmed by love.

10 June 1973

A layman comes to the monastery with great yearnings and hopes. He is full of zeal and enthusiasm to work and worship and to serve everyone in love, but all of these lovely things fade in a few months or years. He then accepts any errand in the city with little hesitation. The reason is that since joining the monastery, he has not fully absorbed the proper monastic spirit. He has not mingled with experienced virtuous elders in order to properly learn the spirit, for monasticism is a mystery. He has deceived himself or was deceived by his father in the monastery with Biblical commandments yet never fully absorbed the spirit of the fathers of the desert and their teachings and guidance. He deviates from the moderate spiritual path.

14 June 1973

The hard shell that protects the fruit for a monk is humility and self denial. That is, to be unknown to others and in doing so, to deny himself and carry his Cross. If a virtue is disclosed it becomes worthless. A monk should therefore be unknown to others, without honour, praise or care. In this manner he guarantees the protection of his soul against the vainglory of the world.

20 July 1973

You can recognise a true monk seeking the Lord by his search and pursuit for the way. By his many questions and his attachment to those who preceded him and walked the same path. But there is great spiritual danger for a monk who only cares about satisfying his superior and fulfilling orders in order to be loved by everyone, thus the Lord says, "Their quiver is like an open tomb; They are all mighty men" (Jer 5:16). St Isaac says, "Let your acquaintance be with those who love goodness so that you might live with them in heaven, because he who has been enlightened can enlighten others."

29 July 1973

Steadiness in patience in one place is the fruit of the ascetic life. The more grace bestowed upon a monk, the deeper he progresses in his spiritual life. It all depends on the atmosphere surrounding him; the soil in which he is growing, the fatherhood, the brotherhood, the noise he is dealing with and living amongst. A spiritual atmosphere full of love, intimacy and peace pleases the saints and brings energy and eagerness bursting forth from them for long periods of time.

30 October 1974

People have the right to choose their spiritual guide. God Himself loves this freedom of choice; He never pushes a person or obliges him to do something against his will, even if it is for his own good.

Peace and happiness go hand in hand with humility and a pure conscience. God dwells in the pure heart that fulfills the commandments.

The confession father of a monk should be a spiritual doctor (familiar with the diseases of the soul and spirit), a spiritual leader (experienced in the wars of the enemy) and a father, with all its meanings of love and kindness. He should also be caring, following the ideal example of our Lord Jesus Christ when He said that the shepherd lays down his life for his sheep and is always ready for sacrifice.

There are many types of crosses, including emotional struggles, physical illnesses, persecution and wars in every shape and form. Every person has their own cross to bear with patience, in awe and silence, until the grace from God allows this cross to be lifted. The person will then receive a full crown, and for this reason the monks are namely called the 'Bearers of the Cross'. How beautiful is it for a monk to carry his cross, whom Christ has placed upon his shoulders, in order to enter His Kingdom, just as with Christ Himself; who had to go through the Cross in order to attain resurection and to conquer death (finally, there is laid up for me the crown of righteousness)

Blessed be the Lord at all times

24 July 1978

Chapter 2

Bible Contemplations

Early Spiritual and Monastic Maturity

This sermon was given by Fr Mettaous to a community of monks, four months after his ordination as a monk in the year 1950.

Dear your grace Bishop Theophilus and my dear fathers the priests and monks of the blessed El Sourian Monastery.

I congratulate you on the feast of the Nativity of our Lord Jesus Christ, hoping that He may return these days in growth by His grace, blessings and heavenly gifts, and may He extend the life of our beloved bishop Theophilus. May He grant him growth in the true monastic life, and may He continue the days of spirituality in his days, through his prayers on our behalf, and his deep love towards everyone, and his great humility that inspires us to be like him. May the Lord extend his bishopric reign for many years to come, spending his days in peace and without harm. Through the pleadings of our Lady the Virgin St Mary and St John Kame.

Your Grace, and my respected fellow fathers and brethren, I seek your absolution and forgiveness before I start my talk, as I see myself unworthy to stand in front of you, or to speak to you, for I am a sinner and a weak man.

However, what encouraged me to give this talk is the fact that I am amid my family. Our father Bishop Theophilus blesses us with his presence. For, as a young child, I was accepted in this family, despite my weakness and unworthy state, to speak to you, dear reverends and monks, in the spirit of love, after taking absolution and blessings from my father:

"Glory be to God in the highest, peace on earth, and goodwill towards men."

The angels orchestrated this beautiful song to the shepherds who were vigilant over their flock. Upon entering the manger, they saw the Child wrapped in swaddling cloths, placed in the manger of livestock.

How wonderful that the Creator of Heaven and Earth, to whom every knee in heaven and on earth worship, would humble Himself to come to earth, to the land of misery, to save the creation broken through the sin of the first Adam.

Great news came to us with His miraculous birth. Sing, O my soul, with the angels with this new praise, and learn, O my spirit, the humility of the Creator of the universe and how He was born in a disdained manger.

Truly, how great are these two virtues, which the Lord taught us, among many other virtues, which are Love and Humility:

Firstly, Love: God is love, and out of His love for us, he came down from His highest heaven to wipe away the sin of Adam, and to make us heirs in His inheritance in the glory of His Father. The Bible mentions that He was a Man of great sorrows and experienced in pain. He shared with us everything, except for sin alone. He lived on earth as a man, and in the end He was crucified, was tortured, was placed in a tomb, and arose. Through His resurrection, He broke the gates of Hell and opened the gates of Hades.

Observe, what we should do in return to such great love? Indeed we ought to seek to attain this great love with all our efforts. As monks, through the grace of God, we despised the world and all its lustful desires; we forsook our parents, relatives and friends, and thought about how to attain such love, and what to sacrifice to attain it.

We sought to come to this holy place, where our saintly forefathers lived, and where they attained the highest spiritual level that one can attain, so that their mind and thoughts were in the heavenlies. For a person cannot look at the world with one eye, and with the other eye observe the heavens.

We have living examples of strong personalities, who left behind footsteps for us to follow, that witness to their greatness in the path which they walked in, that is, monasticism.

Monasticism: its sweetness is in its bitterness, and its beauty is apparent. It is delicious to eat; its glories are in heaven. Even though it has many tribulations in its path, and its struggle is difficult, yet when we lift our eyes to the heavenlies, all this pain on earth is worth it.

Therefore, my brethren, let us seek to attain the true love of our beloved Jesus, so that our yearning and enthusiasm may increase, and may the strength of the Lord support us and guide us by His grace.

"My grace is sufficient for you, for My strength is made perfect in weakness."

Secondly, Humility: I am in awe! How can the creation contemplate that the Lord of glory – who spreads out His hands and feeds every living creature – would be born in a disdained and rejected manger. He even said: "Foxes have holes and birds of the air have nests, but the Son of Man has nowhere to lay His head." This was said to teach us a great lesson.

Occasionally I would look at my weak self, when an evil thought bothers me, and I say to myself: "what are you thinking about, poor man? Look at the dust, for it is your mother, and from it you were created, and to it you will return. But look at the prince of the dark hosts, and what rank he was in before he became proud and fell forever."

The Bible mentions the forefathers in their prophetic words, inspired by the Holy Spirit, that without humility, we cannot increase in our spirituality one single step, and therefore we would never reach our goal of the heavenlies.

"Looking unto Jesus, the author and finisher of our faith"

"Whosoever looked upon Him were enlightened, and their faces shall not be ashamed"

We raise our hearts to the Child in the manger, through the prayers of our father Bishop Theophilus – who is a role model for humility – asking God to make us true monks, not just by names, struggling in every virtue with all holiness, godliness, love and humility. May we be worthy to enjoy the heavenly glories with all the saints who struggled and conquered.

Through the pleadings of our Lady the Virgin St Mary, and St John Kame, and all the saints who have pleased you since the beginning with their good deeds. Amen

Happy New Year

From the mouth of the most despised and youngest monk.

7 January 1950

The Last shall be First

"For the kingdom of heaven is like a landowner who went out early in the morning to hire laborers for his vineyard. Now when he had agreed with the laborers for a denarius a day, he sent them into his vineyard. And he went out about the third hour and ... Again he went out about the sixth and the ninth hour... And about the eleventh hour he went out and found others standing idle... and he gave them their wages, beginning with the last to the first...But when the first came, they supposed that they would receive more; and they likewise received each a denarius. And when they had received it, they complained against the landowner... So the last will be first, and the first last. For many are called, but few chosen." (Matt 20: 1-16)

The Lord told us a parable about a man who had a vineyard, who hired labourers for his vineyard. One team started at the first hour, another at the third hour, another at the sixth hour, and another at the ninth hour. Finally, he found idle people at the eleventh hour, so he sent them to work in his vineyard. He had a agreement to pay them one denarii each at the end of the day. We note that the people who got paid first were the last people to come to work, at the eleventh hour, and were made equal with those who started working from the morning.

It might be that the Lord of glory wants to teach us that cursed is the man who does the work of the Lord in vain. The people who came at the eleventh hour, are the people who come into the faith late, and their faith and good deeds bring forth fruit, and become a salt to the earth and a light to the world in a short period of time, and so deserve to receive the good reward like the people who were born in the faith from a young age, and who struggled all their lives to attain the Kingdom. We also hear in the history of monasticism of youth who struggled and excelled beyond elders in virtue. Did not the right hand thief deserve the Kingdom of Heaven, while the disciple perished, despite excelling beyond other believers in the Lord Christ?

The Lord also teaches us about jealousy and envy, which develops in our hearts when we see others excelling in their deeds, and for this reason it was mentioned in the parable that the workers complained against the landowner. The Lord carries the sins of mankind, but He cannot stand jealousy and envy from a man. Disgruntlement indicates their unacceptance of what the Lord has in place for them, which means they are going against the will of the Almighty Lord. It is as if he wants to be in charge of his own life. "Is it not lawful for Me to do what I wish with My own things? Or is your eye evil because I am Good?"

So the "last will be first, and the first last". The Lord also said: "By your patience possess your souls." The life of solitude on this earth is a life of continual struggle with continuous enthusiasm, for monks have been called to this life from the Landowner, to praise and bless and glorify Him continuously, so that they may not deviate from the temptations of the enemy, that they may not lose the path to Heaven.

10 September 1956

❧ ❧ ❧

"I am the door. If anyone enters by Me, he will be saved, and will go in and out and find pasture." (John 10: 9)

Jesus is the door. Whoever finds Him will be saved, and whoever enters by Him, will go into the deep, and will not reach the bottom of the Lord's consolance and unspeakable mercy.

Is this pasture not the pasture of our fathers the saints, who ate from it, and lived in it, and gave us of its fruits as teachings to fill us? The souls of His beloved find pasture in Him, and they contemplated on the One whom they love, until they understood the secrets of the Kingdom of God, and so they were drunk with His love. They forgot the body, and its pride; not only their thoughts, but their souls transcended up to heaven. They knocked on the door, and the Bridegroom quickly got up to open the door to welcome His bride out of His great love towards her. He could not wait, He was waiting for a groan. There they were filled with the Living Spring that does not run dry. The Lover asked her, 'what do you seek?' (till now you have not asked anything in my Name) Then she took from Him and after that, when she was saved and delivered, she overflowed on others with this treasure of goodness.

9 January 1957

※ ※ ※

"And when He had looked around at them with anger, being grieved by the hardness of their hearts, He said to the man, "Stretch out your hand." And he stretched it out, and his hand was restored as whole as the other." (Mark 3: 5)

Is this not evidence for obedience? Just the fact that the sick man obeyed the order of the Lord, by stretching out his hand, his hand was healed.

Therefore, obeying the commandments has the power to heal the illnesses of the soul.

9 February 1957

※ ※ ※

"But He said to them, "It is I; do not be afraid." Then they willingly received Him into the boat, and immediately the boat was at the land where they were going." (John 6: 20-21)

When a person is far away from Jesus, he will be scared and in despair. The empty heart, which God has not reigned over yet, is like a boat in the midst of the sea. But when we open the door for the One standing outside knocking, He will come in and immediately we have reached the harbour of peace and comfort.

13 April 1957

A Fiery Love

Blessed be our God, who redeemed us with His honoured Blood on the cross, thus we were allowed to enter the Holy of Holies in Heaven. That is, through our faith in Him, we were reconciled with His Father, and thus became partakers in the glory. Being sinners , we sought to be set free from the bonds of sin, but we could not. But suddenly He shone inside our hearts with His light, and the darkness was scattered, and His strength set us free from the bonds and so not out of righteous deeds did we attain this freedom, but through His mercy He freely saved us.

The ways of salvation are many, and the ways of asceticism are diverse. Whoever sees a ray of light in his heart, he immediately struggles and forces himself to increase in his level of spirituality and holiness.

The monks have seen and heard many stories of the struggles of great saints, such as St Anthony, St Paul the Hermit, St Bakhomious, St Macarius, and St Shenouda who used to crucify his body on a cross like his master throughout Passion Week. St Paul of Tammouh and St Bishoy, as well as others who worshipped God with their hearts, were enlightened, and thus were able to shine as an example to the generations to come, and to us at this present day.

Many times we would cool off, and try to imitate them, wanting to be like them, but far be it! We forget, or neglect, that these great saints, who fended off the devils and their unseen traps, had a greater goal; their goal in life was 'Love'. How deep is love, even though it is little in letters, but is life in its fullness. All the writers of this world, and even the spiritually enlightened, could never fathom the depth of love with their own understanding, or with their pens. For love is God, and who is able to contain God, or speak about God? For God is love.

Those people had a burning fire in their hearts, kindled with their love towards Jesus Christ, and so they kindled their works, so that this verse applies to them: "to him who has, more shall be given".

For this reason, prophets came and prophesied. For this reason the commandments were set, and for this reason we were saved as Christians. For this reason our apostles preached and lived the word of God.

The most convincing answer, for anyone who seeks the life of complete surrender and positive struggle is given in the Lord's answer to the lawyer who asked Him which commandment is the greatest? It is: "You shall love the LORD your God with all your heart, with all your soul, and with all your mind.' This is the first and great commandment. And the second is like it: "You shall love your neighbor as yourself.' On these two commandments hang all the Law and the Prophets." (Matt 22: 37-40)

22 May 1957

Is it greed, or the ambition of the soul?

A person is never satisfied in material things for as soon as he achieves something, he starts looking for another target. Sometimes he even tries to leap hurdles in order to reach his aim, when in reality he destroys himself and loses everything. There are two factors related to this: fear and doubt. Fear compels a person, while doubt makes him confused between truth and certainty, and so he stands still and is confused, but remember the words of the Lord "I wish he were hot or cold, but he is lukewarm" (Rev 3: 15).

So, who can reach the harbour peacefully, without deviation? It is the person who doesn't care about the fears and doubts surrounding him. As long as he is sure and comfortable that he is headed steadily for his target, nothing can hold or frighten him. He is always peaceful during the time of war, his heart is enlightened and he is full of inner comfort because he is heading towards his target, God.

This monk is similar to the tortoise that reached the top of the hill before the rabbit. One of the saints said: "I like consistent light work more than vigorous work that would exhaust me quickly and lead me to soon stop." St John Saba once said: "consistent work, even if it is little, is considered as a great treasure which accumulates."

How great are the Lord's mercies! He never abandons those who seek Him and are submissive to His will, "They looked to Him and were radiant, and their faces were not ashamed" (Ps 34:5).

In the midst of darkness He lights our inner soul, dispelling the darkness and dismissing fear. The Lord Christ once came here and asked, "Why are you toiling here?" I answered, "I am toiling seeking You, Lord, but You are hiding!" Oh, I cannot bear such happiness!

9 June 1957

Then He said to her, "Your sins are forgiven." And those who sat at the table with Him began to say to themselves, "Who is this who even forgives sins?" Then He said to the woman, "Your faith has saved you. Go in peace." (Luke 9: 48-50)

The blind whinged against the Lord when He said to the sinful woman, who annointed His feet with fragrant oil and wiped them with the hair of her head, 'Your sins are forgiven.' Their disgruntlement was from within their hearts, but He who knows the secrets of the heart. They did not know Him, and so they thought they were righteous in their own eyes. On the other hand, she fully knew Him and that He is the One who saves and gives life, and so she received forgiveness.

When the Lord Jesus knew their thoughts, He did not address them, but rather turned to the sinful woman and spoke to her saying, 'Your faith has saved you.' This was to teach them that faith is the rock that might be shaken, and that anybody that falls on it might bruise, but on whom it might fall, it would crush them.

This was His response to the sinful woman, not only to confirm that her sins were forgiven, but to shine a light on the path for everybody to see. Holy and blessed is He forever.

21 June 1957

The Lord ordered Moses to offer sacrifices of only clean animals, forbidding any unclean animals on His holy altar, so that He could smell the sweet aroma of the offering, and be pleased with humankind. This same thing happened with Noah after the flood. The first thing he did after leaving the ark was to offer a sacrifice to the Lord from among the clean animals. Thus, he deserved to hear God's promise that He would never flood the whole world again.

It is the same with prayer. Our prayers are accepted as a sacrifice and as sweet incense reaching Heaven if they come from a pure heart, but if they are mixed with ungodly thoughts, then we are offering unclean sacrifices on the altar of the Lord. God accepted Abel's sacrifice and rejected Cain's.

3 July 1957

꿈〉〉 ꙮꙮ 〈〈

The Presence of God

"And He who sent Me is with Me. The Father has not left Me alone, for I always do those things that please Him." (John 8: 29)

This is what the Lord Jesus said while He was in the treasury, teaching in the temple. We can learn from this that we are continuously present before God, feeling His presence and existence in us and with us. We ought to keep His commandments, and do according to His will, as He dwells in the pure souls and hearts. This is the ultimate, immeasurable joy. How miserable is the life of a solitary monk when he loses the condolences of others, and does not feel any consolance in his own heart. He is then an easy target for the battles of the devil, and there is no helper, because he has not found the pearl of great value.

There must have been a certain object, or sin, which he could not forsake completely, or sell to buy the name of the Lord Jesus, who is highly priced, remembering that "where [our] treasure is, there [our] hearts will be also". How important is the feeling inside a monk that he is in the continuous presence of God, and so a dialogue runs between him and God at all times. Wherever he is, his heart is always praying and repeating the name of our Lord Jesus Christ, asking His forgiveness and guidance, and contemplating His beauty and powerful works. His life becomes consumed with the Lord in everything and in all things, and so he can say "He is with Me, the Father has not left Me alone."

15 July 1957

❊   ❊   ❊

Our mother the Orthodox Church has strong pure pillars, purified by the blood of the Lord Jesus. The Coptic Orthodox Church believes that Jesus Christ is the Son of the Living God incarnated from the Virgin St Mary through the dwelling of the Holy Spirit in her womb. He came to the world to release us from the slavery of the devil, after the fall of our father Adam and after the death penalty was laid upon him for disobeying God, which resulted in his expulsion from Paradise and his toiling on earth. Therefore all of his descendents became subject to this death penalty, as a result of their father Adam's disobedience.

After 5500 years, the Lord Jesus Christ came to restore Adam, and those souls who had departed, to their original rank. Jesus Christ came to free us all. When He gave up His pure soul on the Cross, Satan came to take His soul, but the strong power and the everlasting Divine Spirit captured and chained him, salvaging those who had been in his grasp since the beginning of time. Those who died in hope waiting for the great day of Salvation and Redemption in order to return to the Heavenly Bosom. The Risen Lord could then say, "I will ransom them from the power of the grave; I will redeem them from death. O Death, I will be your plagues! O Grave, I will be your destruction! Pity is hidden from My eyes" (Hosea 13:14).

This is what Jesus Christ did for us, what then have we done for His sake? O my Lord, we stand in great shame and You are so merciful. Help us to despise this vain life and this perishable body, and to place our souls in Your hands. Do whatever You wish with me, according to Your will. Will you send me to the slaughter, to jail, or to be tortured? I am yours, My Lord, You have purchased me with Your precious blood. I simply ask You to sustain my weak faith. I cannot say my heart is ready my Lord. My heart is not ready, for without You I can do nothing.

Simon Peter dragged a net to land with 153 fish in it, yet the net was not broken (John 21:11). The net is the church, which embraces all her children of all nations. She endures their weaknesses and mistakes, praying for the salvation of all, and that they all come to the knowledge of the truth. She never dismisses a sinner who approaches her in repentance and never forsakes a wicked sinner seeking refuge from the evil world. She is never torn or weakened.

25 July 1957

❧　❧　❧

"For the iniquity of the Amorites is not yet complete" (Gen 15:16).

Often we see the wicked living happily and enjoying life's luxuries, while the children of God are experiencing many temptations. We all know that God is the Almighty just judge. He is only bearing with the sinners until it is their time of judgment and their casting into Hell, thus realising the fruits of their evil deeds and their life away from God.

17 August 1957

❧　❧　❧

"Be faithful unto death, and I will give you the crown of life." (Rev 2: 10)

I have fought the good fight, I have finished the race, I have kept the faith. Finally, there is laid up for me the crown of righteousness." (2 Tim 4:7,8)

As monks we ought to be honest, and honesty requires a lot of struggle and repentance. We also need to be steadfast, always recalling the early zeal that led us to monasticism. This is something that continues until our last breath, not only for a number of days or years. If a person is given the choice of denying his faith or withdrawing his holy convent, of course he will offer himself up for slaughter or surrender his body to all kinds of torture, but will not deny his aim in life, "...looking unto Jesus, the author and finisher of our faith." (Heb 12:2).

The issue of honesty is very serious and important in our lives. Through it we achieve our hope of obtaining a strong weapon to fight the traps of the enemy, who is never weary and fights us all the time. We must be honest to the end in our love for the Lord and our neighbour, and be honest in our humility, our illnesses and our tribulations.

Finally we must be very honest during our separation from our Heavenly dwelling unto the last breath.

22 August 1957

※》 ※☾☽℀ 《※

"And whatever you ask in My name, that I will do, that the Father may be glorified in the Son." (John 14:13).

We can do everything through our Beloved Jesus Christ. When we ask the Father in the Name of Jesus, who united us with the Father and is the Only Begotten Son, He will provide us with what we ask for. As St Paul teaches us through his Epistles, which are full of grace, "I can do all things through Christ who strengthens me" (Phil 4:13); "In the name of Jesus Christ of Nazareth, rise up and walk'" (Acts 3:6). There are also many other verses proving that there is no other name by which we can be saved except that of the Lord Jesus Christ.

Through Him we were saved from our sins, and by His pure Blood and glorious Resurrection we will enjoy the eternal joy of the Heavenly dwelling. Thus, whoever believes in Jesus Christ has eternal life, and whoever does not will be judged and the wrath of God will fall upon him.

As Christians, we owe a lot to that Great Name. What have we offered to Him who loved us and laid down His life on our behalf? Are we exchanging love with Him? If we could fully comprehend the grace and mercies that Jesus Christ is giving us, we would offer Him our lives, and consider that dying for Him would be appropriate.

But how can we do so unless we receive power from Him first? Thus He will be the One working within us and through us for the Glory of His Blessed Name, "If you love Me, keep My commandments. And I will pray the Father, and He will give you another Helper, that He may abide with you forever - the Spirit of truth, whom the world cannot receive, because it neither sees Him nor knows Him; but you know Him, for He dwells with you and will be in you" (John 14:15-17).

7 October 1957

※※ ※※※※※ ※※

Moses the Prophet ordered the children of Israel to keep the Lord's commandments saying, "And these words which I command you today shall be in your heart. You shall teach them diligently to your children, and shall talk of them when you sit in your house, when you walk by the way, when you lie down, and when you rise up. You shall bind them as a sign on your hand, and they shall be as frontlets between your eyes. You shall write them on the doorposts of your house and on your gates" (Deut 6:6-9).

It is amazing how strict and accurate we must be, even precautious, lest anyone should sin out of negligence or reluctance in fulfilling the Lord's life giving commandments.

Woe to us Christians, and especially the monks, if we fall short of fulfilling our Lord's commandments. The Lord Jesus says that if we break one of these commandments, we break them all. He also says, "You can do nothing without Me." Yes, His commandments are not heavy, but who can be saved if he depends on his own personal struggle alone? We are in great need of the Lord's grace, especially in these spiritually dry times where life is more complicated and evil is increasing. Our enemies, especially the hidden ones, surround us everywhere to trap us while we are unaware. Had it not been for God's mercies, they would have destroyed us.

So we should always plead, persist and ask for our Heavenly Father's help. He does not wish that any one of us should perish. We must always remember His commandments and depend on Him for their fulfillment, "Jesus answered and said to him, 'If anyone loves

Me, he will keep My word; and My Father will love him, and We will come to him and make Our home with him'" (John 14:23). Our aim in life should revolve around loving God and the foundation of our life should be Love.

We worry and are very careful not to upset our Lord if we sin, but how can we keep ourselves from sinning when sin is in our nature? We can do so by keeping His commandments, which in themselves have great power that helps us fulfill them. We have salvation in the great Name of the Lord Jesus Christ, so let us love Him from the depths of our hearts. Whatever we are doing, let our lips speak this Holy Name without ceasing, repeating with St Paul, "For I am persuaded that neither death nor life, nor angels nor principalities nor powers, nor things present nor things to come…can separate us from the love of God" (Rom 8:17) .

He is Holy and Blessed at all times.

20 October 1957

❯❯❯   ❮❮❮   ❮❮❮

"Woe to you when all men speak well of you, For so did their fathers to the false prophets" (Luke 6:26). The Lord did not mean that we have to commit sin to avoid being praised, but when we fulfill His commandments we will face obstacles. We will have to choose whether to speak and act according to the divine commandment, ignoring those who resist us, or whether we give up the commandment in order to keep our worldly dignity and be praised by others.

The Lord Jesus says, "I do not receive honor from men" (John 5:41). People accused Him of many things: "Now when the Pharisees heard it they said, 'This fellow does not cast out demons except by Beelzebub, the ruler of the demons" (Matt 12:24), and it is the same with the sons of God, the saints, the disciples, the martyrs and the ministers of the Word. They were all persecuted for witnessing for the Truth. St Athanasius was told that the whole world was against him, but he answered that he was against the whole world, because he was sure he was following the way, the truth and the life.

174

I used to think that this saying contradicted the verse which says, "Let your light so shine before men, that they may see your good works and glorify your Father in heaven"(Matt 5:16), but then my mind was enlightened with this verse, "Woe to you when all men speak well of you, For so did their fathers to the false prophets" (Luke 6:26). The false prophets would tolerate people in their sinful deeds and crooked ways of thinking, depending on their position as prophets, while in reality they were false prophets and their father was the devil, the liar and father of liars. Therefore these false prophets were honoured in the eyes of the people and always received their praise.

In the Old Testament, the same thing happened with Micaiah the Prophet and Ahab the King of Israel, who listened to the false prophets (1 Kings 22).

"A disciple is not above his teacher, nor a servant above his master" (Matt 10:24). The war between what is true and what is false, between light and darkness, purity and impurity, and between what the soul desires and what the body desires will not cease. "But Peter and the other apostles answered and said: 'We ought to obey God rather than men'" (Acts 5:29).

19 November 1957

※》   ※(🙂)※   《※

"And everyone went to his own house, But Jesus went to the Mount of Olives" (John 7:53-8:1). All of the Scribes and Pharisees, those who gathered to judge Jesus, returned to their homes. They returned because they cared only about their bodies, their comfort and their enjoyment of a life of luxury. Their thoughts were worldly and their rest was in a house of clay. They did not know the eternal house built without hands, nor the way that leads to it. They refused to know the way, the truth and life. Shame on them, for they did not know that the day would come when their hypocrisy would be disclosed openly. They returned to their homes to think of new evil tricks to accuse the innocent.

But Jesus went to the Mount of Olives

Jesus went to the Mount of Olives to speak to His Father about the darkness and injustice of humanity, pleading for them to know the way that leads to eternal life. Jesus' resting place is never in houses because, "Jesus said to him, 'Foxes have holes and birds of the air have nests, but the Son of Man has nowhere to lay His head'" (Matt 8:20). Jesus did not go to a house to eat or drink or sleep. He went to the Mount of Olives, where He had another form of food not known by the chiefs of evil. His food was to do the Father's will, which was the salvation of every soul.

Caring for the soul is life, but caring for the body is death. The Chief of Life went to the mountain where there is life for the spirit. Our disturbed soul escapes from the world's troubles and noise into the wilderness where the soul is healed of its illness, and the mind and heart is purified. In the wilderness the spirit is lifted up and becomes sublime through unity with its Creator. After Jesus struggled with the people, He went to the Mount of Olives to continue His spiritual struggle with the Father through prayer, for prayer is the beginning and completion of every good deed.

14 December 1957

※ ※ ※

"Now there were in the same country shepherds living out in the fields, keeping watch over their flock by night. And behold an angel of the Lord stood before them, and the glory of the Lord shone around them, and they were greatly afraid. Then the angel said to them, 'Do not be afraid, for behold, I bring you good tidings of great joy which will be to all people. For there is born to you this day in the city of David a Savior, who is Christ the Lord'" (Luke 2:8-11).

While the fox Herod was in a deep sleep after indulging in luxurious desires and while the Scribes and Pharisees were deceiving people, depending on their knowledge and position, here, in the open fields we see the shepherds keeping watch all night, caring for their flock. These poor watchful shepherds were the only ones who deserved to hear the first annunciation about the birth of Jesus, the hope of Israel, whose birth the prophets prophesied hundreds beforehand. The children of Israel were waiting impatiently for the birth of their King and Saviour.

The angel of the Lord appeared to these simple shepherds revealing the good news, comforting them, assuring them not to be afraid but rather to be happy and rejoice because the fullness of time had come. The Saviour of Israel has been born to save His people and illuminate the darkness. What a great joy for those captured in Hades to know that their Saviour was finally coming to save them! "How beautiful on the mountains are the feet of him who brings good news, who proclaims peace, who brings glad tidings, who proclaims salvation..." (Isaiah 52:7).

Simple pure souls like those of the shepherds deserve this grace over others. Blessed are the watchful shepherds because they will give an account for their flock on judgment day. They should never think that they are toiling in vain. Let them take comfort from the shepherds who watched their flocks all night, even though they were in an open area, with no fences to protect them, with enemies around them on every side, and a cloud of witnesses surrounding them.

7 January 1958

❧ ❧❧ ❧

Every person should have his share of suffering and tribulations allocated by God. Who can flee from His Face? "Where can I go from Your Spirit? Or where can I flee from Your presence?" (Ps 139:7) Sometimes a person can complain about being in a certain place and think, "If I go somewhere else, I will be happy," but in fact he will find the same or other types of pain wherever he goes. So victory comes from patience, "By your patience possess your souls" (Luke 21:19). Our life on earth is all about falling and rising, "For a righteous man may fall seven times and rise again." (Prov 24:16).

So St Paul the Apostle says, "Do not be haughty, but fear," (Rom 11: 20) because it is written, "conduct yourselves throughout the time of your stay here in fear," (1 Peter 1:17) "redeeming the time, because the days are evil" (Eph 5:16). We need to cling to the Lord Jesus and live with Him in real love and intimacy so that He can be our comforter in tribulations and temptations, and our victory in hardships until we meet Him in heaven. We say this with St Paul, "Yet in all these things we are more than conquerors through Him who loved us" (Rom 8:37).

He is Holy and Blessed at all times.

20 January 1958

>>> ※※※ <<<

"Then they drew near to the village where they were going, and He indicated that He would have gone farther. But they constrained Him, saying, "Abide with us, for it is toward evening, and the day is far spent." And He went in to stay with them. Now it came to pass, as He sat at the table with them, that He took bread, blessed and broke it, and gave it to them. Then their eyes were opened and they knew Him; and He vanished from their sight. And they said to one another, "Did not our heart burn within us while He talked with us on the road, and while He opened the Scriptures to us?" (Luke 24: 28-32)

The Lord appears many times as if He is walking away from us, and we feel a drought in our souls, and we do not usually know that we are the cause, because we did not ask for Him. He yearns to dwell in His house (the soul) because He said, "Behold, I stand at the door and knock. If anyone hears My voice and opens the door, I will come in to him and dine with him, and he with Me" (Rev 3: 20). This teaches us that we ought not to be silent, nor stop purifying our hearts, so that it will be an acceptable upper room for the Lord. Then what happened, "they constrained Him, saying, 'Abide with us'". Here, we do not let go of Him, we cling onto Him like Jacob did when he said, "I will not let You go unless You bless me". We force Him to enter into His new dwelling place, and to purify it according to His good will, for when He enters, He feels the dryness of the soul, and so He fills it with His grace and feeds it with His love. Now it came to pass, as He sat at the table with them, that He took bread, blessed and broke it, and gave it to them. When the soul is fed with His Body and Blood, it becomes drunk with His love, and forgets everything around it. Only then will our hearts eyes be opened, and will the mist of darkness vanish from around the soul, and only then will we begin to feel as if we were in Heaven for "the kingdom of God is within you", and so the soul will receive consolation and will be able to fight and conquer the enemy.

The Holy Fifty Days 1957

The Lord Jesus says, "The wind blows where it wishes, and you hear the sound of it, but cannot tell where it comes from and where it goes." (John 3:8). This is a beautiful simile for the hidden work of the Holy Spirit within human beings.

St James the Apostle says, "My brethren, let not many of you become teachers, knowing that we shall receive a stricter judgment" (James 3:1). This statement corresponds perfectly with the teachings of the early Desert Fathers who lived the life of celibacy and solitude.

Once a novice asked an elder monk what he should do to live as a true honest monk. The elder did not preach or explain Bible verses. He just answered, "Stay in your cell and it will teach you everything." The novice did as he was told and he found great comfort in his spiritual life.

As for this generation in which we are living, with so much technology and knowledge, faith has weakened and consequently, the work of the Spirit has decreased because of the many obstacles resisting its work.

There are so many sermons conducted, thousands of preachers, many educated people, plenty of books and authors, but we find that we are living in a generation which cares for the outer appearance which has very little spiritual depth.

Why do we often deceive ourselves? Why do we care more about the outer appearance than the inner? I am afraid we are the "whitewashed tombs" of which our Lord spoke of. This is happening because we have deviated from the path of our early fathers and are rushing to listen to different teachings, and trying to find a quick fix for our broken souls. We are not giving the Spirit a chance to work within us in tranquility and peace. This only happens when we submit totally to God.

Seal the door of your struggles with silence, lest the tongue destroys it.

The great Saint Isaac taught deep, precious spiritual teachings about silence and serenity and the important role they play in being filled with grace and replacing the old man. He lived during the sixth century and would describe his generation as lukewarm and promiscuous, so what can we say about the generation of the twentieth century? Can we find the kind of silence that St Arsanius described as being able to be broken by the sound of a bird?

4 August 1958

※ ＊＊＊＊ ※

"But as many as received Him, to them He gave the right to become children of God, to those who believe in His name" (John 1:12). What a great honour it is for us as Christians to be called the children of God. This phrase may be said easily and taken for granted, however if we examine it under the strong light of grace, we will realise how precious this honour is. The great Almighty God, the Creator of everything, the unlimited, calls us His children! A father can understand how strong the feeling of love is for his children.

We are the children of God. How awesome and joyful it is to become children, and to know we are no longer slaves. If this is the case, why do we fear tomorrow and what will happen after? The Lord has previously promised us that He will look after us as a Father full of love and kindness, so why worry?

"For God so loved the world that He gave His only begotten Son, that whoever believes in Him should not perish but have everlasting life" (John 3:16) and "See, I have inscribed you on the palms of My hands; Your walls are continually before Me" (Is 49: 16).

He also says that whoever touches you, touches the apple of My eye, and even if a mother forgets her nursing child, I will never forget you.

We trust His promises, so we should be strong in our battle against evil because we are the children of the great King. No matter how grievous our sins are, His mercies are greater, "and my delight was with the sons of men" (Prov 8:31). St Isaac said that He silences the noise of those in heaven in order to listen to the cries and pleas of the human beings who are praying. Let us be strong and steady, and cry out in deep sighs:

O Abba, Father, through our Beloved Saviour Jesus Christ, please do not forget Your creation that You have shaped with Your own Hands. You know our weak nature; we need Your continuous support and help.

6 August 1958

⋙ ᾿ᾞᾭᾭᾦ ⋘

Monks often feel that their spiritual fervour in worship is weakening. This is because we usually use only words, not deeds. For example, a monk might say, "I will start a practice of seclusion, silence, and remaining in my cell," and all kinds of similar practices. If he faces a struggle from the devil or feels boredom, he may fall backward and sink into deep depression, but after so much toil he will be back where he started.

Monasticism is the path to repentance and also the path to death. Our life should be moving forward, not backward. We must be patient until the last breath and when our Lord sees our patience, He will quickly send help and support. Let us leave expressions such as 'spiritual exercises' and 'spiritual retreats' to lay people who are struggling in the world and need spiritual retreats and sessions to revive themselves spiritually. As for us monks, monasticism is a stable continuous way of life, as long as we keep carrying the cross. Let us continue this until death, following our Master's example.

As a setback occurs in a sick person before he is completely healed, the same happens in us before we are totally free from the old man. For while we are heading forward, we then suddenly fall, giving the evil one a chance to mock and goad us with more fierce fights. We must continue to be patient.

As long as we are still alive we need to be steady in our humility. If we have not completed our service properly, we should wait patiently until we are completely convinced to perform it without doubt or interruption. We should not do this in haste so that we do not fail and become a subject of gloating for our enemies. The proof of this is the strong and stable work of the Spirit within us, "for without Me you can do nothing" (John 15:5).

Monasticism is a ladder on which monks ascend step by step in order to reach perfection, but if they try to jump or skip some steps, they will simply fall to the bottom and so they must be patient, supported by the grace of God, Who tolerates their falls and always endures their weaknesses.

May the Lord have mercy on us all and help us obtain the salvation of our souls.

26 August 1958

There is a hidden battle with the devils because the soul is in pain due to previous sins. If the soul does not completely get rid of the old man, then it will be in conflict with those bad habits, with whom it compromised itself with before, and so will fall into sin as a result.

"Be sober, be vigilant; because your adversary the devil walks about like a roaring lion, seeking whom he may devour" (1 Peter 5:8). Sometimes the soul falls into deep distress and confusion after intense prayer or meditation, as if it is really fighting and struggling with a hidden enemy. But while experiencing this, the soul is depending on the power of faith in its strong tower: Jesus Christ. "The name of the Lord is a strong tower; The righteous run to it and are safe" (Prov 18:10).

In the midst of its fierce struggle, the soul can feel the support of its beloved God whom it is yearning to reach, but which it is prevented from doing so by the guards of darkness. It then feels such peace and comfort and in a blaze of love, therefore it pleads in tears to its beloved Lord Jesus, repeating with the Psalmist "My heart is ready O God," and thus sees all pain as nothing for the sake of this love.

Blessed is the soul that pays its debt willingly while here in the flesh, instead of facing tortures unwillingly in the place where there is no hope and remorse is useless.

The Lord says: "without Me you can do nothing" (John 15:5), also, "'Not by might nor by power, but by My Spirit,' Says the Lord of hosts" (Zac 4:6). So who would dare say that it is because of my courage or piety that I am repenting to face the war with the mighty ones and win salvation? No way! If we are not supported by the Lord's grace, and are not depending on Him or believing in His love, there is no salvation without His Holy Name.

We are so young, our Lord, we do not know the narrow way. We are weak and hopeless, and not as strong as our early fathers who successfully completed their struggle in the blessed call to monasticism. We only depend on your true promise, "Assuredly, I say to you, whoever does not receive the kingdom of God as a little child will by no means enter it" (Mark 10:15). Let us live and stand before you as innocent young children and simple fishermen, hoping to be embraced by Your divine love.

2 October 1958

※   ※(⊙)※   ※

Then the king said to me, "What do you request?" So I prayed to the God of heaven. And I said to the king, "If it pleases the king, and if your servant has found favor in your sight, I ask that you send me to Judah, to the city of my fathers' tombs, that I may rebuild it." (Nehemiah 2: 4-5)

This is the way the men of God are in life; their lives become continuous with the Lord, they receive help and guidance, and their prayers are heard and answered. They live all their lives in His presence (even though He is near to everybody).

"Then Elijah said, "As the LORD of hosts lives, before whom I stand" and St Paul said: "I was praying to God...", while he was in the middle of a conversation. How much more ought the monks be, who have consecrated their lives to this internal world? How can their souls be liberated from the heaviness of the body, to soar high with Christ and be in His presence forever?

If I do not confirm myself in the truth, until I become an inseperable part of Him, then it does not avail me. For all the honoring I receive from others now, and whatever I enjoy from the lusts of this world will end, either by life or death. And then I look at myself, and I am empty inside. Empty from all consolation, where it comes from true peace. Empty from all the works of grace that girds me in tribulations and wars, the hidden and the manifest. Empty from the continual connection with the true spring that does not run dry, and from where the soul seeks its fruit and is nourished.

And then suddenly I realise that the days and years have passed by and I am still ignorant and I still think I am walking, until I stand in front of the fearful throne of God, and I am naked and in shame and disgrace, and others can see my shame, and where regret is no longer an option. Your mercy O Lord.

17 May 1959

The Lord of glory said to the sinful woman who wiped His feet: "Therefore I say to you, her sins, which are many, are forgiven, for she loved much. But to whom little is forgiven, the same loves little." (Luke 7: 47)

And we know from the teachings of the saints that a person cannot attain the level of true love if they do not first control reverence. But in the story of the sinful woman, we see that the Lord describes her: "for she loved much", whereas when she came to Him, she was in the peak of her sins.

It is truly amazing that our Lord Jesus, our Great Shepherd, who left the ninty nine sheep and went to look for the one lost sheep, who was eating with the sinners and the tax collectors, said that "I did not come to call the righteous, but sinners, to repentance." Therefore, there is no barrier between us and Him, because He yearns towards sinners. Thus there is joy in the presence of the angels of God over one sinner who repents.

And to receive salvation, He looks upon the keeness of the heart and the emotions of love towards Him, which pour out in front of him with silent groaning, silenced by the beastly lusts, overcoming the weak human willpower, which could not find another way to escape from sin.

It is for this reason the Chirst of glory came to our world to break our bonds and to shine in our darkness and heal our souls' pains. We are indebted towards His great Name, without which there would be no salvation.

The first commandment is love, and it is the foundation of all constructions.

Indeed in other spiritual aspects, love is the highest level, and whoever attains it would have attained the top of all other virtues. O great love, full of delicious fruit because you are the pure vine. Draw me closer to the Beloved, so that I may forget my ego and forget my past life, and come under the feet of the Master, to listen to the word of salvation coming out of his blessed mouth; cleansing me from the original man, and granting me everlasting life by offering a pure repentance and through the renewing of the spirit through holiness. Thus in my days of estrangement, my thoughts, hopes, yearnings and emotions are in the Kingdom of Heaven, where my beloved sits amid the praising of the Cherubim and the Seraphim and all the Heavenly Hosts. There I might be counted to participate in the praising and rejoicing without ceasing that does not run dry. Everytime I shout with them, my soul yearns more and my love increases for Him who loved me first. I want to calm down for a little while, but love draws me closer and rekindles in my heart a stronger flame, and thus my soul would continuously be in a relationship with Him.

If I live on earth, my soul belongs up in Heaven. O great love, how magificent and how majestic are you, for God is love.

El Sourian Monastery

23 July 1959

My soul yearned to converse with the spiritually enlightened, and those who have tasted the gifts of the spirit, and to learn from their paths, and how they reached such a spiritual level. How did they transcend and go beyond the realm of this world, and soar high in the heaven of the spirit. How did they knock on the door, and it was happily opened unto them, as they became full in the spirit.

My soul yearns for those who searched diligently to receive the Kingdom of Heaven and its righteousness, who earnestly searched for the hidden treasure inside of them, for their lives are from Him, in Him and to Him they will return. My heart earnestly yearns to be in union with their hearts, to attain the same goal.

There is no doubt that the monastic path needs extensive guidance by a spiritual advisor, and for experience in the same spiritual realm, from someone who has already tried it. Experience about its internal and external warfares, points of weakness, traps set by the devil, and how to overcome them with the weapons of God, among other matters. How accurate is the life of a monk.

1 August 1959

Denying One's Self

"Then Jesus said to His disciples, 'If anyone desires to come after Me, let him deny himself, and take up his cross, and follow Me. For whoever desires to save his life will lose it, but whoever loses his life for My sake will find it'" (Matt 16:24,25). I can see that monasticism is based on this: denying yourself, carrying the cross and sacrificing your soul (surrender, sacrifice and total death).

It is not easy for a person following the path of virtue and God's commandments to deny himself. How wonderful it is though for a person to achieve this virtue of self denial, for it contains a great degree of humility. How can we deny something that is already existing, being the ego, and let Jesus Christ live within us so that He becomes the one working inside us and with us, for the glory of His holy Name? As for my soul, which has put me in so much trouble, it enjoys the praise of people, leading to its destruction. If it is humiliated or passed over, it becomes angry and envious, and starts to avenge itself...

- The soul that wants to have the biggest share and highest level of praise and compliments does so because of its pride and conceit, while "for he who is least among you all will be great" (Luke 9:47,48).

- It does its best to be famous and well known, and if it can't achieve this openly it puts on a veneer of piety and holiness to gain praise. "Woe to you when all men speak well of you" (Luke 6:26)..."having a form of godliness but denying its power." (2 Tim 3:5)

- Jealousy and envy: If the soul notices that someone else is being praised or honoured, it tries to attract this praise to itself and if it fails, it starts to belittle the praised person in order to attract all eyes to its own fake virtues. When it fails, it envies and feels resentment internally, becoming like a boiling pot.

- The pain of adultery is one of the basic reasons for feeding the ego and is also preceded by pride and haughtiness.

- Murmuring and judging, even audibly, is also a sort of love of the ego. If I consider myself as one who is despised - as said by David the great prophet and king, who was anointed by God but called himself a worm and a dog - then why do I judge others and want to be above everyone else? This is due to a lack of love.

- Also concerning my outer appearance: clothing, walking, sitting amongst other things. Why am I so proud of myself? Why talk about what I have done all the time, as if I am the Creator? Yet

I am leading my poor soul to total and permanent darkness…

• What is the remedy for all of these pains inside me? The Lord answers in a simple manner: deny yourself, carry the cross every day, and forget about yourself. It is a matter of denying yourself first, then carrying the cross and forgetting yourself. These are very clear, strong, straight-forward words… (John 12:24)

16 August 1959

※ ※※※ ※

"But tarry in the city of Jerusalem until you are endued with power from on high." (Luke 24: 49)

This was the instruction given to the disciples by the Lord before they received the Holy Spirit to go out and preach. For had they been sent to preach but were not given the Holy Spirit, then they would have failed in their preaching. We can apply this verse in our lives for the people who consecrate their lives as monks to live an ascetic life, either by locking themselves up or generally those who are in solitude in a cave in the mountains. They ought to live first in the community of the monks (Konpion), completing the works of obedience and humility under the guidance of an experienced father of confession, to be filled with grace and to train up in virtues until they receive spiritual strength to fend off the devil, and so they would be counted with the victorious in every battle. The Lord will battle for them, and not through their own weak power.

7 December 1959

※ ※※※ ※

In the miracle of feeding the five thousand with the five loaves and two fish, there was clear evidence for God's greatness, who was able to work so much through the weakness of many, to make them strong. If His grace creates something out of nothing, then He is able to do absolutely anything. The number ONE is the beginning of all numbers, and a THOUSAND is the completion of numbers, and so are the tens and hundreds. Thus it is written "one day is as a thousand years, and a thousand years as one day".

It is as if the five loaves were enough to feed the five thousand, at the rate of feeding one thousand people with only one loaf. Blessed be our God who is able to feed our hungry souls when He sees the readiness of our hearts, and our struggle to keep all His commandments and to listen to His voice. When our own strengths fail, according to His good will, He gives us grace and feeds and renews our souls. Glory be to God forever.

8 January 1960

꙰   ꙰   ꙰

"Because the Spirit is truth" (1 John 5: 6)

St John is teaching us that when a person always speaks the truth, senses the truth and lives with truth and in truth, such a person becomes spiritual because he is filled with the Spirit, and the Spirit has started to work through him for the glory of God.

"And you shall know the truth, and the truth shall make you free." (John 8: 32)

If we do not abide in the Spirit, how then can we know the truth?

For this reason we hear Christ talking to Pontius Pilate: "I am a king. For this cause I was born, and for this cause I have come into the world, that I should bear witness to the truth. Everyone who is of the truth hears My voice." Pilate said to Him, "What is truth?"" (John 18: 37-38)

We see that, because Pilate was empty from the spirit, he could not understand the truth, or know it, because he does not believe in Him, therefore whoever is born of the Spirit is spirit, and the man who walks according to the Spirit knows the Spirit, because in Him we live and move and have our being (I am the way, the truth and the life). However, the misleading spirit of this world is Satan, and for this reason Christ said about him that he is a liar and the father of it, and lying is the opposite of truth, "we are in Him who is true, in His Son Jesus Christ. This is the true God and eternal life." (1 John

5: 20)

21 July 1960

※※　※※※※　※※

"Now when He got into a boat, His disciples followed Him. And suddenly a great tempest arose on the sea, so that the boat was covered with the waves. But He was asleep. Then His disciples came to Him and awoke Him, saying, "Lord, save us! We are perishing!" But He said to them, "Why are you fearful, O you of little faith?" Then He arose and rebuked the winds and the sea, and there was a great calm." (Matt 8: 23-26)

"The Kingdom of God is within you", "you are the temple of God and the Spirit of God dwells in you".

Here we see the remarkable power of our Lord, which requires strong faith, for if we believe that God is dwelling inside of us, then eveyone of us should get inner consolation. No doubt that the Lord is here with us and He fills us from inside, but many a time we go through the same tribulation that the disciples went through here, where the strong waves of tribulation and temptation strikes us, and our strength is quickly drained, and we feel overwhelmed, desperate and alone. At this moment, our faith's eyes are diminished, and we forget that the name of the LORD is a strong tower; the righteous run to it and are safe.

1 August 1960

※※　※※※※　※※

"He who loves father or mother more than Me is not worthy of Me. And he who loves son or daughter more than Me is not worthy of Me. And he who does not take his cross and follow after Me is not worthy of Me. He who finds his life will lose it, and he who loses his life for My sake will find it." (Matt 10: 37-39)

Monasticism is based upon this foundation. It is great love, which starts off with reverence, and is consumated by love of Christ who loves me and has strengthened my love for Him, and overcame my

190

love for my father, mother, brother, sister and everyone else. Even though I love those people in Christ, but my love to them is not as great as my love to Him, for His love transcends above all hearts and the ability to think or understand.

There are pains and sorrows in the path of love, and just as our beloved Saviour carried the cross and showed His utmost love, thus the servant is not greater than his master. For if He, being righteous, bore pain and suffering for our sakes, how much more ought we to carry our own cross and to die daily for His name's sake.

"Whoever finds his life will lose it." Thus if we do not die to ourselves, we cannot live. What is truly remarkable about the monastic path, is that whatever I desire to do, I should do the exact opposite. If I want to save my body from sickness, I should instead sacrifice my body to keep my soul.

Therefore, monasticism is death to the soul before death to the world. I die, so that Christ may live within me, and what St Paul called 'taking off the old man', and this is not attained except through the gift of God, after being steadfast in the path, until grace visits you. So be patient, O you who struggles.

4 August 1960

※ ❦ ❦

"Then the kingdom of heaven shall be likened to ten virgins who took their lamps and went out to meet the bridegroom. Now five of them were wise, and five were foolish. Those who were foolish took their lamps and took no oil with them, but the wise took oil in their vessels with their lamps." (Matt 25: 1-4)

From this we learn that the ten virgins were equal in stature in that they all kept themselves pure and chaste, but the wise ones exceeded the foolish, because they took oil in their vessels, but the foolish ones were content with the oil already in their lamps.

They did not think ahead, that their oil would eventually run out, due to it burning out, and that they would eventually need more oil in case it does run out, so that the lamp may stay lit.

The wise virgins considered this, and it is for this reason that the gospel mentions them by being wise, where wisdom has built its house. The oil in the lamp is the good deeds and pure thoughts that spring forth from a pure heart that is fervent with love towards Christ our Lord. They are constantly ready to meet the Bridegroom, and so they were not content with keeping their virginity, but they constantly cared about fulfilling the commandments, from love and forgiveness to humility, faith, hope and long suffering, and so they were always in constant growth in the love of Jesus, firm in the vine, flowering and bringing forth the fruits of the Spirit, some 30, 60 and a hundred fold.

"But the wise took oil in their vessels with their lamps." Therefore, when the Bridegroom came unexpectedly, they were quick to fill their lamps to be ready to meet the Bridegroom, and so they were considered worthy to enter with Him into the Heavenly wedding.

The Lord made us ready and vigilant to fulfil all the commandments, and not to be content with being just monks, and so letting go of the control of eyes, thoughts and feelings, or failing to subject the body, as it is written, "for whoever shall keep the whole law, and yet stumble in one point, he is guilty of all" (James 2: 10). Let us receive aid from Him, for alone we can do nothing. May His mercy be on us, through the intercessions of St Mary and all His saints. Amen

11 August 1960

※ ❦ ❧

"Now behold, two of them were traveling that same day to a village called Emmaus…But their eyes were restrained, so that they did not know Him…Then their eyes were opened and they knew Him; and He vanished from their sight." (Luke 24: 13, 16, 31)

Sometimes it might appear to one who walks in the path of the Lord that he is walking in complete darkness. He wants to see any spiritual scene, or yearn to hear the voice of God to be consoled and encouraged to endure his pains and sufferings, but he walks as if in the dark. He does not realise that the Lord is very close to him. However, He hides Himself for a good purpose. And then suddenly he realises the presence of God only when He allows it. Therefore it is not out of our own personal effort that we feel the Lord, but rather it is the work of grace in the right time, according to His own good will.

18 September 1960

⋙ ❦ ⋘

"In the sweat of your face you shall eat bread" (Gen 3: 19)

Blessed be our merciful God. How sweet is the bread of hardships, and how tasteful is the bread obtained after hard work. In so doing, a man fulfils the words of God after he fell, that he has to eat bread in the sweat of his face. It is for this reason that early comfort on earth has nasty and unpleasant effects on its person, both physically and spiritually.

If we apply this matter to a monk who wants to live in solitude, but has not completed the work of the community, most often he will be unstable and nervous.

St Philoxinus explained this matter when he quoted the story of the people of Israel who tasted bitterness and servitude in Egypt as slaves, and then afterwards they were let free in the desert to worship God.

St Paul also mentions the physical and then the spiritual food. Physical food is needed to stay alive, but the Lord Christ called Himself the living Bread which came down from Heaven, for He is the spiritual food, without which we cannot survive spiritually.

We need to attain this spiritual food inside us, and to unite with Him, and to become the dwelling place of God, for without Him we can do nothing. We ought to struggle and fight in the path of repentance, because it is a narrow path. We ought to be patient to save our souls, putting on the new man, so that He might give us our inner food and comfort.

Monday 15 November 1960

"Then the LORD appeared to Solomon by night, and said to him: "I have heard your prayer." (2 Chron 7: 12)

How excellent is it when God hears our prayers. It is the wish of every creature on earth, and it is the end of the struggle of every struggler who seeks perfection, and it is also a sure sign of the love between a son and his father, who walks according to his will.

How can a monk attain this level, of having his prayers heard by the Lord. To my knowledge, it is impossible, unless he fulfils the commandments of the Lord, because the effective, fervent prayer of a righteous man avails much. How can we be righteous, if we are sinners and have no righteousness within us. Yes, we can do all things through Christ who strengthens us, because He is our righteousness and He completes our weaknesses. For this reason we ought to be attached to Him until the very end, to be confirmed in Him and Him in us, and thus we can bring forth fruit of the spirit. This will happen if we remain steadfast in the vine, otherwise we will wither away and be cut off.

However, how to pray is a great matter, because not every man who stands and recites a few words has prayed, but indeed prayer has many paths, and different exercises, limitations and qualities, because it is the food of the soul and it is also a gift of the Spirit. Let us ask God to grant us true spiritual prayer, which is heard by Him, and not only heard, but also answered, according to His good will.

God hears all the groans of the soul, before He hears our words. He examines our depth, and knows all things.

If we want our prayers to be heard and answered, it is truly a marvelous thing.

Elijah was a man with a nature like ours, and he prayed earnestly that it would not rain; and it did not rain.

I pray that I have the ability to keep writing about this topic, but the beginning and the end are in His hands.

May He be blessed forever, forgiving our sins, and hearing our pleadings.

31 December 1960

What is the benefit if I begin to do a good deed, but am stopped

"But the ones that fell on the good ground are those who, having heard the word with a noble and good heart, keep it and bear fruit with patience." (Luke 8: 15)

Our Lord spoke about the virtue of patience, for every action and every struggle, if it is not crowned with patience, avails nothing.

"By your patience possess your souls"

What is the benefit if I begin to do a good deed, but am stopped by an obstacle or through the temptation of the devil, and I stop doing this good deed? I have lost my goal, and thus have failed to complete the good deed.

If we contemplate on the struggle of our forefathers the monks, we see that they tasted the bitterness at the start, and tribulations persisted with them, along with the temptations of the devil, for years. In the end, we hear their testimony that they received comfort and inner peace. This comfort and peace is a state of renewal of the Holy Spirit of their hearts, working in might and strength to confirm them, as in the day they received the Holy Spirit in Baptism.

We, the Christians, have received the gift of renewal of our old man in the Holy Baptism, and through the Confirmation of the Mayroon, but when we walk in the world, our flesh is tempted by the lusts of the flesh and the pride of life overwhelms us. Above all of this, the envy of our enemy does not stop or cease to tempt us, and set traps for us to deceive us and drag us away, so that everyone has received the punishment of resisting God Himself.

Instead of being temples for His Holy Spirit, to dwell in our hearts, we willingly accepted to deviate and resist God's work in our hearts, and the Holy Spirit who we received in the day of Baptism. We accepted to be led by the devil to live in sin and to do according to the will of the evil one.

"When a strong man, fully armed, guards his own palace, his goods are in peace. But when a stronger than he comes upon him and overcomes him, he takes from him all his armor in which he trusted, and divides his spoils." (Luke 11: 21-22)

If we want to defeat this mighty enemy, which is sin, we ought to uproot it and cast it out of our hearts, and to prepare our souls to return to its correct use, which is to be the dwelling place of the Spirit of God, and to bring forth fruit of the fruits of the Spirit which love, joy, peace, long-suffering, kindness, goodness, faithfullnes, gentleness and self-control. (Gal 5:22)

It is for this sole reason that monasticism arose, and was founded on this principle – the principle of repentance. Our forefathers built their spiritual life on this strong foundation; for monasticism is death – with all the meaning of the word – and for a monk to reach the state of renewal, he needs to be patient for his whole life, and therefore patience becomes the most important virtue to remain steadfast and to bring forth fruit, and later to receive the eternal life, as without holiness no one will see the Lord. Glory be to God forever.

16 September 1961

※》 ※※ 《※

True Christians

"Not everyone who says to Me, 'Lord, Lord,' shall enter the kingdom of heaven, but he who does the will of My Father in heaven" (Matt 7:21).   Our Lord Jesus Christ teaches us that it is not enough to repeat words, many or few, such as, "Lord, Lord". I can also say that even perpetual prayers are not sufficient to enter into the Kingdom of Heaven. In saying this I am not belittling prayer, which is our shield and our source of strength and support, however there is danger in becoming accustomed to repeating our prayers just to complete an order. The Lord came and was incarnated to teach us important things, so we can enter His Kingdom by His great mercy and not because of any goodness within ourselves, "The thief does not come except to steal, and to kill, and to destroy. I have come that they may have life and that they may have it more abundantly" (John 10:10).

The Lord taught us His holy commandments and taught us that they are not heavy. Though we have to enter through the narrow gate and go through many hardships and tribulations, when compared to the apparent pleasure of sin that leads to total destruction on earth and eternal condemnation.

If we consider all of the sufferings of our saintly fathers, we will see that they witnessed for the Lord in many different ways, each according to his spiritual stature. Thus they forgot their pains and felt joy, even during their suffering, for the sake of the Beloved One. It is clear that as Christians we are not of this world, for if we were then we would be submissive to the chief of this world and comforted by his material things that pass away. On the contrary, we are the children of Light, surrendering in joy to our Heavenly King, our Lord Jesus Christ who purchased us with His precious blood. We must act in a manner that pleases Him in this life, fulfills His will from the depth of our hearts, depends on His power, and asks for His support. For without Him we can do nothing.

25 January 1962

☙ ❦ ❧

"But remember me when it is well with you, and please show kindness to me; make mention of me to Pharaoh, and get me out of this house." (Gen 40: 14)

When Joseph was in prison, and he interpreted the dream of the butler, he asked him "remember me when it is well with you, and please show kindness to me; make mention of me to Pharaoh, and get me out of this house." And indeed the dream was fulfilled and the butler went back to his position, and the Bible mentions "Yet the chief butler did not remember Joseph, but forgot him".

This happens with us frequently. We forget the good deeds and mercies of our Lord, which He treats us with, and when we are in a hardship our prayers increase dramatically, and we vow and pray fervently for God to deliver us from this hardship.

And when God bestows upon us with relief, we forget everything. We are taken away by our worries about the world and pride of life, and we forget what we vowed to God and others.

For this reason, St Paul taught us, saying: "but exhort one another daily, while it is called "Today," lest any of you be hardened through the deceitfulness of sin" (Heb 3: 13).

How often does man forget good gifts! We always need to remind ourselves that we are indebted to God for His unimaginable love towards us, and His gentle association with us, as He did not judge us according to our sins, but instead has showerd us with immense grace.

We are also in debt to our Christian brothers, because what God has bestowed upon me, whether gifts, money, work or blessings is not for me, but rather is a treasure of goodness which He has made me ruler over to distribute to others. For out of His goodness we shall give Him back.

We can contemplate on this story from Joseph's side as well. What does he say: "For indeed I was stolen away from the land of the Hebrews; and also I have done nothing here that they should put me into the dungeon".

The planning of God is truly marvelous and wonderful, for He exalts whom He wants, and puts down whom He wants. He lifts the needy out of the ash heap, so He may seat him with princes and He has put down the mighty from their thrones, and exalted the lowly.

God has chosen people everywhere, and He knows them and He tests them with the fire of tribulations to purify and exalt them, to prepare them for a certain job. The Holy Bible is full of examples of prophets, apostles and saints. These people experienced very dark days, to the point that they thought they had ceased to exist, and yet the eye of the Lord was merciful and His mercy kept them alive, even in the midst of a fiery furnace, or with vicious lions, or in seas or prisons.

Joseph was innocent, sold by his own brothers. He could have told those who bought him that it was his own brothers that sold him, and maybe he would have been saved. Yet he did not, but he totally relied on the valiant hand of the Lord, and he left matters in His hands.

He was sold as a slave, and served Potiphar with all honesty. He was tempted with the harshest temptation faced by any youth. It was so harsh because it was persistent, day after day. But because he was hiding in the stronghold of the Lord, keen to complete the commandment of the Lord, His commandment protected him from falling in sin, whose fallen are all of great stature and whose injured are many.

In the end, his reward was being thrown in jail unfairly. He could have defended himself from this false accusation, but he did not. It is as if he wanted to drink the cup of suffering until drunkenness, like his Lord our Christ. During all of this, no miracle occurred from Heaven to get him out of jail, and yet he was patient for the heavenly verdict.

"But even if you should suffer for righteousness' sake, you are blessed", and this happened because his heart was filled with divine peace, which is the reason for fulfilling the commandments of the Lord. Even when he was in prison, he felt deep peace because the Lord was with him. In contrast, the evil person does not have peace within him, and so even if they are on thrones with great people, they will not have peace.

We see the inevitable result of such patience and endurance, that God took him out of prison and raised him and made him ruler over all of the land of Egypt, and he was the reason for the survival of thousands of people, including his own father and brothers.

How great, then, is the virtue of patience, enduring the pain and suffering of temptations and tribulations that attack us from both human beings and from Satan, as well as the pains of the person themselves! As long as the person persists and struggles, and does not give up, then God will allow the day to come when all these pains and struggles are healed, and He will unbind us from the bonds of sin from Satan, and will mortify our sinful desires. Thus we will feel that we are taken out of prison and are able, through the grace of God, to bring forth eternal fruit, and a great inheritance with those who loved Him and have pleased Him with their good conduct, and through acts of mercy and compassion. Glory be to God forever. Amen

19 February 1962

※ ✵❀✵ ※

"Then the priests, the Levites, arose and blessed the people, and their voice was heard; and their prayer came up to His holy dwelling place, to heaven" (2 Chron 30: 27)

"Your prayers and your alms have come up for a memorial before God." (Acts 10: 4)

"Cornelius, your prayer has been heard, and your alms are remembered in the sight of God" (Acts 10: 31)

"Thus says the LORD, the God of David your father: "I have heard your prayer, I have seen your tears" (Isa 38: 5)

"I have surely seen the oppression of My people … and have heard their cry … Now therefore, behold, the cry of the children of Israel has come to Me." (Exo 3: 7-9)

How beautiful is it when our prayers are heard before the Lord, and our prayers enter His dwelling place! This is the desire of those who love Him with all their hearts, who struggle all their lives to fulfil all His commandments to live in His sight in straightness of heart and purity of the soul, until He looks down upon them and hears their cries, and unbinds them from the bonds of the devil, both hidden and manifest. Then they will praise Him continuously in joy and delight. This will allow them to ask and they shall be heard in the day of their trouble, and so He will come and save those who trust in Him.

Blessed is our beloved Lord Jesus who saves our souls, and who humbled Himself to come into our world to save us and unite us with Him.

Now I ask myself, are my prayers heard in His dwelling place? Or has it become a routine? And if so, then what are the ways to purify my prayers to be acceptable before Him? To my knowledge, nothing pleases God more than to see the purity of the heart of man, for it is the source of life for the body, and it is also a spiritual spring bringing forth life to feed the soul. Therefore man ought not to say I am a layman, or a monk, or a priest or a bishop. God does not look at the outer appearance like we do, but He examines the heart and knows the intentions. If priesthood is the promoted and elect people before God in church, then monasticism is consecration of the whole life to God.

I fear that, having been called a monk and priest, I would become a stumbling block to others. People might think more of me than what they can see, when God sees everything inside of me, and might have a different judgement of my character.

St Isaac the Syrian said that work saves a man, regardless of its shape or name.

Therefore, let us pay attention to purifying our hearts and souls from the pains of the original man, and through the grace of God, may we be renewed by the work of the Holy Spirit, who gave strength to the disciples on the day of Pentecost. May our souls become the dwelling place for Him, who makes intercession for us with groanings, which cannot be uttered, remembering the verse "You are the temple of God and that the Spirit of God dwells in you", may our prayers ascend to heaven as sweet aroma to the dwelling place of the most High God. And may the Lord accept us to Him, and hear our prayers, and may He be the subject of our joy and delight.

But be aware, lest we fall to the commandments of man, and stumble in fulfilling the commandment of our Lord. Let us be alert, for many have lost their path in making the means as a goal... "to the Jews a stumbling block and to the Greeks foolishness".

May the Lord protect us from the right hand blows, because the path of simplicity is a sure path.

Glory be to God forever

Sunday 4 March 1962

"Therefore be patient, brethren, until the coming of the Lord. See how the farmer waits for the precious fruit of the earth, waiting patiently for it until it receives the early and latter rain. You also be patient. Establish your hearts, for the coming of the Lord is at hand." (James 5: 7-8)

A monk struggles from the very beginning, in fastings and vigils, prayers and prostrations, humility and obedience and in serving the community of monks, in solitude and isolation, and he begins to long for the presence of the Lord to fill him with consolation and grace, and he awaits the divine gifts, which he has read about in the books of saints such as St Isaac the Syrian or St John Saba.

He yearns for the higher spiritual levels, which he has heard of, and all of this in a few years. He expects to reap the fruit before the seed dies in the ground.

Poor is this man, if he is a layman struggling in the path of the Spirit in the world, or if he is a monk who seeks solitude and serenity.

We hear the words of St James, "be patient" which is a beautiful word, which requires a lot of deep contemplations, because great are the mistakes of wanting to rush things in the path of the Lord, and so He teaches us to be patient. The incarnation of the Word, and His coming into our world is a great example of patience, because He was patient for five thousand years before He perfected the plan of salvation. If we rush, and we ask for something that is not in its right time, it becomes a transgression against the divine plan of God, because we might be asking for something at the wrong time, which might be harmful to us.

But God, who does exceedingly abundantly above all that we ask or think, knows what is best for us, and He gives us in the right time as it pleases Him, who stretches out His hands to feed all living creatures. "See how the farmer waits for the precious fruit of the earth, waiting patiently for it until it receives the early and latter rain." This is true in the science of vegetation, because a fruit that develops too early is weak and is worthless. St Isaac the Syrian said, "every gift that comes without effort, consider it as a still born child, that has no life in it". The quicker it comes, the quicker it goes away. Therefore, remain steadfast in hearts and know that the coming of the Lord is close.

It is very important that we remain steadfast in keeping the commandments of the Lord, and to love Him with all the heart above all things, not looking forward to His gifts and rewards, otherwise our love will be for a hidden purpose. These gifts come naturally; and He is honest in His promises, for when the heart is purified, the gifts come of their own accord naturally; just as a magnet attracts a metal piece, thus the soul that awaits the coming of the Bridegroom and His dwelling in it. Let us remain steadfast in Christ, wherever we are, and however we are, whether we are in the darkness of the soul, or in boredom and weariness, and even if we have no consolation in any shape or form. Our Lord is merciful, for He shines from time to time in the soul of His beloved ones. These visitations are a testimony of His love to the devout and honest soul, until the time comes when He will come and dwell in the heart, and then the person will feel like he was taken up to heaven, even while his body is still on earth. This is the renewal of the Holy Spirit.

This comes after a long time of struggle, battles and tribulations, which test the honesty and love of those who seek the Lord with great hope. Everything is given according to His will and through the divine grace.

"Every good gift and every perfect gift is from above, and comes down from the Father of lights, with whom there is no variation or shadow of turning." (James 1: 17)

19 March 1962

※⟩⟩ ⁂⟮☉⟯⁑ ⟨⟨⟨

"Manasseh was twelve years old when he became king, and he reigned fifty-five years in Jerusalem. But he did evil in the sight of the LORD, according to the abominations of the nations whom the LORD had cast out before the children of Israel. For he rebuilt the high places ... he raised up altars for the Baals, and made wooden images; and he worshiped all the host of heaven and served them. He also built altars in the house of the LORD...And he built altars for all the host of ... he caused his sons to pass through the ... he practiced soothsaying, used witchcraft and sorcery, and consulted mediums and spiritists. He did much evil in the sight of the LORD, to provoke Him to anger. He even set a carved image ...So Manasseh seduced Judah and the inhabitants of Jerusalem to do more evil than the nations ... And the LORD spoke to Manasseh and his people, but they would not listen...Now when he was in affliction, he implored the LORD his God, and humbled himself greatly before the God of his fathers, and prayed to Him; and He received his entreaty, heard his supplication, and brought him back to Jerusalem into his kingdom. Then Manasseh knew that the LORD was God... and commanded Judah to serve the LORD God of Israel." (2 Chron 33: 1-16)

Holy is our gracious God, and patient on the sinners, for He desires all men to be saved and to come to the knowledge of the truth. We see in this story how Manasseh sinned greatly against God, and defiled the House of God, and submitted to the will of the devil blindly, as the Holy Bible says about him: "he practiced soothsaying, used witchcraft and sorcery, and consulted mediums and spiritists. He did much evil in the sight of the LORD, to provoke Him to anger." Thus he brought with him thousands of people to sin against God.

He truly lost the way, and was difficult to be saved. However, in the life of King Manasseh, the power of repentance and humility is beheld, and the fact that tribulations are allowed by God to alert His sons who have strayed away, to be vigilant and to return to God with repentance, for their sins to be forgiven and wiped away. That they may return to the stronghold of God, fleeing from the evil one who has bound them with iron fetters to strip them away from the grace of God. When they are unbound, they would offer true repentance and remorse for their past sins, with a broken heart, to receive salvation.

Repentance brings forth sons who are renewed, and tribulations alert the slumbered souls, so welcome the tribulations sent by our caring and merciful God, for the rod of a gentle father on his son is to teach him, but is gentle not to kill him, and as David the Psalmist says: "Try my mind and my heart."

The sins of King Manasseh were too many to list, which exceeded all levels of sin, and it did not just stop at him, but extended to the people of Israel, he "seduced Judah and the inhabitants of Jerusalem to do more evil than the nations", and the Bible mentions that whoever makes one of these little one stumble, it would be better for him if a millstone were hung around his neck, and he were drowned in the depth of the sea. How much more does Manasseh deserve, then?!

"Therefore the LORD brought upon them the captains of the army of the king of Assyria, who took Manasseh with hooks, bound him with bronze fetters, and carried him off to Babylon. Now when he was in affliction, he implored the LORD his God."

He was lost in darkness and the enemy had hardened his heart against his Lord, and Manasseh insisted in provoking God. However, God was patient on him. He was able to wipe him away in a moment of time, but He waited to make Manasseh an example to all generations, to show His servants that He opens His arms wide open to accept all sinners who return to Him with repentance.

We knew from His Gospels that He is merciful and patient beyond all understanding, "a bruised reed He will not break, and smoking flax He will not quench". When the sinful woman was caught in the act, and was brought to Jesus to condemn her, what did Jesus say? "He who is without sin among you, let him throw a stone at her first". When everyone was heavy burdened with their own sins, nobody could cast the first stone, and so one by one they began to leave, fearing that their sins may be made public.

Jesus said to the woman, "Woman, where are those accusers of yours? Has no one condemned you? She said, "No one, Lord." And Jesus said to her, "Neither do I condemn you; go and sin no more." Thus, He teaches us that His mercy and patience on sinners is to allow them to repentance.

Our merciful Lord knows our human weakness and that we are normally inclined to sin and evil, and so He set the path of repentance for us to reach Him. Beware of lingering too long away from the right path, because He said if you fall, then rise again, and He is waiting at the door knocking, and when He sees us coming to Him from a far distance He runs towards us to receive us and accept us back to Him. He would then clothe us with a new garment, because we were dead and now we are alive, and we were lost and now have been found. Heaven rejoices at the repentance of one sinner.

20 March 1962

❧ ❀ ❧

"You shall love the LORD your God with all your heart, with all your soul, with all your strength, and with all your mind." (Luke 10: 27)

If we love God from all our hearts, souls, and strength, then how can we love Him with all our minds?

I think that our Lord Christ meant that we should gradually increase our love for Him, until we reach the love from all the mind. This is the highest level, and saints and hermits lived in this stage where they would live in the joy of the Lord in their waking hours, during sleep, when eating, during work and when walking.

This is what the fathers meant by the expression 'controlling the mind'. They attained this level after living for long years in great struggle with their own nature, and with devils. They struggled until the blood and death, with the enemy who wants to separate man from his Creator.

This is the degree of completeness, which they refer to as 'crucifying the mind'. They told us, regarding it, 'whoever is crucified has accepted purging of the sins of the original man, and from the wrath of God which was destined for him.' Thus they were indeed correct.

There is no doubt that there is a risk in controlling the mind in such a manner, for a person who lives in the world, or for a monk living in the monastery, if they have no proper guidance from someone who is more experienced in this struggle, and who has been given grace.

When a student asked his teacher about continual prayer, he replied, "rejoice, my brother, that continual prayer is reached by those who have reached a state of completeness, through which they can appreciate its value. It will come of its own accord, because it is written, 'the Spirit Himself makes intercession for us with groanings which cannot be uttered.'"

St Paul also teaches us, "bringing every thought into captivity to the obedience of Christ," (2 Cor 10: 5) and I think he means that we ought to cast out every evil thought that does not agree with the commandment of the Lord. This implies that we ought to have the commandments before us as a mirror to measure up to the will of the Lord.

We should, therefore, begin by saying that we should love God from all the mind, if the only thought and the strongest thought is the love of God, which dominates all other thoughts. And we can stop here.

However, if we explain the meaning of the love of God from all the mind literally, then we ought to add continual prayer, which we mentioned earlier. Continual prayer must be followed by 'crucifying the mind' always before the Lord, which we have not yet received from the grace of God. How can I love God without praying to Him, because prayer and reiteration are the bonds of divine love! I think that this level would not be given to a person who is always worried about materialistic things, nor to a beginner monk. However, as St John the Short said, "the baskets are for the camel, the baskets are for the camel" because his mind was subdued by God, that he forgot what the man asked of him.

25 March 1962

⫸ ⫷

"The LORD is with you while you are with Him. If you seek Him, He will be found by you; but if you forsake Him, He will forsake you." (2 Chron 15: 2)

"Because you have forsaken the LORD, He also has forsaken you." (2 Chron 24: 20)

The Lord sent Shemaiah the prophet to Rehoboam and to the leaders of Judah and said to them, "You have forsaken Me, and therefore I also have left you in the hand of Shishak "(2 Chron 12: 5) and thus we see that the Lord is honest in His word, that He will be with us as long as we seek Him, but if we neglect His commandment, then He will deliver us into the hands of the enemy, for a while, to realise that we can do nothing of our own, because in Him we live and move and have our being.

When we feel that we are distant from Him, and we feel the power of temptation, and that we can do nothing on our own without Him, we cry out with Jonah the prophet from the belly of the fish. Since the Lord is near, and He examines our depths, "For the eyes of the LORD run to and fro throughout the whole earth, to show Himself strong on behalf of those whose heart is loyal to Him" (2 Chron 16:9), He hears our cries and listens to our groans, He sees our tears and He comes down and delivers us in various ways. He delights our hearts and comforts our souls, until we receive peace that we have lost, and reconcile with our great God with the covenant of repentace and returning to him. The more we humble ourselves to eat from the pods of the pigs, which does not fill our hunger, we will realise that we belong to Him as His sons and daughters.

We learn a valuable lesson for the future; that we ought to ask for assistance and to be in continual vigil from the traps of the enemy towards our weak nature and our inclination to sin. We ought to remain steadfast in Him, holding on to Him, as we enter with Him into our hearts, and to dine with Him.

Our souls would be comforted and His love will mesmerise us, so that we are in continual communication with him, whether we are sleeping or are awake. We say to Him, "I am my beloved's, and my beloved is mine. He feeds his flock among the lilies." Thus, if we eat or drink, we are alive with Him forever. Glory be to God forever.

29 October 1963

Fruit of Virtue

"The righteous shall flourish like a palm tree, He shall grow like a cedar in Lebanon. Those who are planted in the house of the Lord shall flourish in the courts of our God. They shall still bear fruit in old age; They shall be fresh and flourishing" (Ps 92:12-14).

Saint Isaac the Syrian says, "Know my son that silence, meaning solitude, and any other virtue gives fruit according to our persistence and patience in practicing it." Continuous work, even if it is small, will bear plenty of fruit in the long run. We are often mistaken in thinking that the path of holiness and the proper spiritual life is a short, easy one and that acquiring more virtues depends on our own righteousness. We think that becoming saints can happen by just imitating the lives of saints... This will actually lead to a life that is spiritual in appearance but not a genuine one. In doing this, we will be completely deceiving ourselves, and after some years, we will lose our initial spiritual warmth and return to lukewarmness. We realise that the flame which we thought was igniting us has been put out, thus resembling the fig tree that had many leaves but no fruit. The Lord Jesus is asking for the fruits of the Spirit within our souls, not just the outer appearance of worship. We should be aware of this so that we do not become like the cursed fig tree.

Abba Agathon was once asked, "Which is the greater, our bodily toil or guarding what is inside?" He answered, "A person resembles a tree: the toil of the body is the leaves but guarding what is inside is the fruit. So, each tree that does not bear fruit will be cut and cast away in the fire." Let us preserve the fruit by preserving our thoughts. We need the leaves to cover, protect and decorate the fruit. I really like the saying by an elder who said, "If you see a youth ascending to heaven according to his desires, pull him down by the feet, because this is more beneficial for him."

We cannot just imitate those who struggled and won, because we do not know the full details of their struggles, their wars with the devils, their falls, their victories, etc., for it is impossible for all of the details of their experiences to have been recorded.

The saints were all ornamented with a very important virtue by which they conquered, that is patience, as it is written, "By your patience possess your souls" (Luke 21:19). The saints bore fruits through their patience. The continuous dripping of water on a rock will make a hole in the rock and so, by patience you can accomplish a great task. Nature which surrounds us is a great teacher of patience, for each thing takes time to grow and become mature, as the Lord mentions in the parable of the mustard seed and how it grows (Mark 4:28). The same goes for the children of God who love and worship Him in Spirit and truth, and withstand all things in patience for His sake. They depend totally on Him when facing temptation or a war from the devil. They are the ones whose spiritual growth progresses in a calm, natural manner, without excessive advances or deviations.

Now we have learned that spiritual gifts and fruits are the result of a long period of true worship and the love of God fulfilling His commandments.

16 May 1966

❧❧❧ ❦❦❦ ❧❧❧

"So it was, when Ahab heard those words, that he tore his clothes and put sackcloth on his body, and fasted and lay in sackcloth, and went about mourning. And the word of the LORD came to Elijah the Tishbite, saying, "See how Ahab has humbled himself before Me? Because he has humbled himself before Me, I will not bring the calamity in his days. In the days of his son I will bring the calamity on his house." (1 Kings 21: 27-29)

This story expresses to us the strength of repentance, and the vast greatness of God's tenderness on His own creation, and that He does not wish death for the sinner, but rather that he may repent and live. And as the common saying says: "we will not be judged for sinning, but rather that we did not repent."

For our life in this flesh, and in this evil world, is constantly under scrutiny and we are always prone to sinning, due to our sinful nature and so it is crucial that we repent daily on our beds of all the sins that we commited during the day.

Blessed is the soul that repents, and is always ready to meet its Heavenly Bridegroom. Also, God is so merciful and patient and He is willing to accept anyone who comes to Him. It is said about Ahab: "But there was no one like Ahab who sold himself to do wickedness in the sight of the LORD" (1 Kins 21: 25).

15 June 1966

≫ ⚜ ≪

The Struggle of a Monk!

It is easy for a person who is struggling to reach perfection to convince himself that he is fulfilling the commandments because he cares more about the outer appearance of his worship than the inner state of the heart. But as for a monk's struggle, he cares about pulling out the pains in his soul by the roots and lives totally with God, without any hurdles or obstacles. In order to reach perfection in Jesus Christ, a monk must love God with all his heart, mind, soul and might and guard his thoughts, for they are the gateway for sin. So he becomes like a soldier carrying his weapon, ready to fight and dismiss the enemy at all times. He never negotiates any thought with the enemy because to do so is to entertain that thought. A monk must remain continually vigilant lest the enemy steal his possessions. I think when the Lord says that we should not sleep; he did not mean the natural rest of the body, because this is a must for human beings. He meant spiritual vigilance, that is, being aware of the enemy and his tricks, because while people are 'sleeping,' the enemy comes and plants his weeds, as mentioned in the Holy Bible. May the Lord grant me a life of watchfulness and help me, for the sake of the salvation of my soul.

20 July 1966

≫ ⚜ ≪

"And everyone who has left houses or brothers or sisters or father or mother or wife or children or lands, for My name's sake, shall receive a hundredfold, and inherit eternal life. But many who are first will be last, and the last first." (Matt 19: 29-30)

"And when those came who were hired about the eleventh hour, they each received a denarius...Is it not lawful for me to do what I wish with my own things...So the last will be first, and the first last. For many are called, but few chosen." (Matt 20: 9-16)

The first set of verses indicates the calling of monasticism, where a monk leaves all his belongings, without any association with anybody, in worship and love with Christ his Lord. He struggles to grow in virtues and in the knowledge of our Lord, and God multiplies His spiritual gifts in this life and makes him inherit eternal life also. However, if he does not remain steadfast till the end, then he will lose everything. If he starts his spiritual life correctly, but then loses enthusiasm and spiritual growth, then he will be delayed, and maybe someone else who came after him would exceed him in spiritual struggle, and inherit eternal life before him.

The second set of verses indicates the serving in the field of the Lord, which are preaching and proclaiming the word of the Lord.

Even though these two sides differ in the way they reach Heaven, but the Lord ends them with the same condition, which is to remain steadfast and in continual growth whilst avoiding slowing down, as He says that God who began with us a good deed, is able to complete it until the end, and the Lord is with us as long as we are with Him, but if we forsake Him, He will forsake us, but He remains honest in His promises, and truthful to those who do His commandments. Let us ask God to assist us in all our struggles.

"Many who are first will be last, and the last first"

24 October 1966

※※   ※（◯◯）※   ※※

"Launch out into the deep and let down your nets for a catch." (Luke 5: 4)

Our Lord Christ teaches us how a faithful servant can catch souls, and return them to the pasture of salvation. We can also apply this to the monastic path, and to those who walk the path of repentance. Thus it applies to those who worship God in Spirit and truth, and who deepen their love for God. They shall never be shaken by the forces of evil, or the temptations of life, however strong they may be.

We ought to deepen our relationship with the Spring of Life, Jesus Christ, and grow in the knowledge of His love, completing all

His commandments in diligence and enthusiasm, until we say with St Paul, "it is no longer I who live, but Christ lives in me" (Gal 2: 20).

Let us beware of vain glory, which is the pest to every virtue, and it destroys the tower of righteousness. Let us enjoy the mocking and ridicule of others, and whatever the devil brings our way to stumble our footsteps, and let us not entertain any thoughts of vain glory. It is not enough to reject it verbally, but we must also exclude it from our souls, even if we do not respond by words to those who praise us, remembering our own sins and mistakes in the past and the present, and also to remember the thought "if the righteous one is scarcely saved, where shall I the sinner appear".

Feast of ascension 30 May 1968

꙳꙳ ꙳꙳꙳ ꙳꙳

"You have become estranged from Christ, you who attempt to be justified by law; you have fallen from grace. For we through the Spirit eagerly wait for the hope of righteousness by faith." (Gal 5: 4-5)

St Paul teaches us that regardless of our works and struggles, they cannot justify us. This does not mean that we should forsake struggling, but that we should not rely on our own righteousness. But rather it is through faith, which strengthens the hope in us and makes us worthy to receive the suffering of our Saviour, who humbled Himself for our sake, and has redeemed us through His Blood, that we are justified. We are saved through relying on His love and guidance, and His truthful promises, because all our struggles are as the dust of the earth. May the Lord have mercy on us.

15 August 1968

꙳꙳ ꙳꙳꙳ ꙳꙳

Let us examine what St Paul said, "if anyone should boast, let them boast in the Lord". Sometimes a person will forget himself and start to talk about himself in matters pertaining to teaching others about his own life that praises the Lord, and in doing so he is asking

213

for the praise of the listeners. This sends the message to the listener that the speaker is either boasting in himself, or that he is asking for glory to be attributed to him. However, we hear of saints who would sit together and discuss the glory of God. They wanted to express the glory of God in their lives, and that without Him, they can do nothing. They have been given grace in earthen vessels, that the excellence of the power may be of God and not of us, so that we may be encouraged to remain steadfast in the struggle in the work of God. In either case, the intention of the speaker is not to attract the praise of the listener, not even mentally, so that if he hears someone praising him, he would be delighted, or be pleased when hearing the praise of others to him in his own mind. He is able to do so by remembering his past mistakes and sins, and how God protected and covered him, and did not expose it to the listeners. These verses should express this meaning more clearly:

"Not walking in craftiness nor handling the word of God deceitfully, but by manifestation of the truth commending ourselves to every man's conscience in the sight of God ... For we do not preach ourselves, but Christ Jesus the Lord, and ourselves your bondservants for Jesus' sake... who has shone in our hearts to give the light of the knowledge of the glory of... we have this treasure in earthen vessels, that the excellence of the power may be of God and not of us." (2 Cor 4: 1-7)

If this principle is unacceptable to many, and especially to beginners, then at least the speaker should have the intention of killing their own ego to glorify God in every word or deed, for in Him and by Him all things are, and in Him we live and move and have our being.

21 February 1970

※》 ※〰〰◌〰※ 《※

"So He Himself often withdrew into the wilderness and prayed" (Luke 5:16).

Our Lord Jesus Christ teaches us how to pray a strong, fruitful and acceptable prayer when we are praying privately, away from anyone or any worldly concern. This cannot be achieved without

214

fleeing to the wilderness. Perhaps the wilderness here means the heart, as the real wilderness has now been settled and filled with buildings, and even the Lord said enter into your bedroom, that is, the heart, and pray to your Father who is in Heaven. The heart should be rid of any other concerns in order to relate to God without hindrance. There is no doubt that the serenity of the wilderness has the great effect of emptying the heart of all concerns and helping it to soar like an eagle, without any worldly burdens that weigh it down or prevent it from enjoying heaven's beauty.

As human beings, how can we liberate ourselves of all of these worldly chains and help the soul reach its Creator? There are so many spiritual practices our early fathers went through, and with the grace of God they achieved their aim. They recorded their experiences throughout their lives, not over a few days like Jonah's plant, until they were able to obtain the Heavenly Kingdom. The grace of God was active in their spirits, so they could achieve salvation. That is why they are called 'saints,' because they are sanctified by Him and their souls are united with His Holiness. The godliness, righteousness, and purity of their lives flowed over others. They are role models in their silence and quietness as they live away from people, yet remain close to them through their teachings and guidance.

Thus the purity of the soul and heart away from the old man is the condition for a strong and accepted prayer, and so a person becomes a temple of God. This is the whole point of our earthly struggle and fight for perfection, in order to inherit His heavenly glories. When we taste the sweetness of the Lord, we should not race onto the spiritual path, but also have the grace of discernment, enlightened by the guidance of the fathers and the Lord granting us His blessings. Therefore we should be wise and preserve this in our hearts, just like St Mary, who kept all those matters in her heart and gave glory to the Lord. And so preserve your treasure, lest you lose it because of your tongue.

5 June 1970

※ ※ ※

"And my speech and my preaching were not with persuasive

words of human wisdom, but in demonstration of the Spirit and of power, that your faith should not be in the wisdom of men but in the power of God." (1 Cor 2: 4-5)

Our apostle St Paul explains to us through these words about the work of grace and the strength of the Spirit in any area, topic, service or life of consecration, and many times we complain throughout these times of spiritual lukewarmness, despite all the sermons and the continual increase in services which are excellent in knowledge and action. This is also true in monasticism, it did not happen a century ago that you would go to a monastery and find so many intellectually knowledgeable monks residing in there, and yet we repeat what St Arsanius said: "the alphabet that a non-educated person knows, he has not learnt it after Arsanius the teacher of the kings' children".

Thus, in the previous verse, St Paul teaches us that the spiritual life in any place or type of consecration, if it is built on human knowledge and wisdom, then it is weak and has little fruit. However, if it was in demonstration of the Spirit and of the power of God, coming forth from a heart full of faith, hope and deep love, then our building will be rock solid and will not be shaken by temptations and pains, but it will increase the strength of its foundation, and will shine with its deep qualities. This type will grow and spread spiritually in quietness and serenity, away from noise or confusion.

However, a soul that is used to feeding on words and discussions, arguments and many teachings, which St Paul mentions regarding the persuasive words of human wisdom, we see that it will often stop along the path, leaning on a weak staff, "for the kingdom of God is not in word but in power" (1 Cor 4: 20). This explains to us the struggle of our early forefathers, whether they are bishops, martyrs or monks, and how they truly were great in their lives, because it sprang forth from a heart full of grace, and so they struggled and conquered, and reached their destination in deep humility. May our Lord give us of their spirit.

20 July 1970

"For we do not preach ourselves, but Christ Jesus the Lord, and ourselves your bondservants for Jesus' sake" (2 Cor 4:5).

How wonderful is St Paul, the great teacher of the universe, apostle of Jesus Christ, chosen by God. He was a true, faithful, humble person, with a pure heart full of heavenly grace as he writes, "who has shone in our hearts to give the light of the knowledge of the glory of God" (2 Cor.4:6). The words "and ourselves your bondservants" highlight the path of humility for the servant, for while he is of the highest rank in the church as an apostle of Jesus Christ, chosen by God to preach His holy name amongst the nations, he denies himself, which is a problem that often becomes a stumbling block to many servants. St Paul did not introduce himself, to those he was to serve, as a distinguished admirable person but rather as their slave; in another verse he says, "Who then is Paul, and who is Apollos?"

How beautiful is the virtue of humility, for it is praised by all the saints. It has the cloak of divinity worn by the Lord Jesus when He was incarnated and took the form of a slave, without which humanity would not have been introduced to, and blessed by the presence of the Lord Jesus Christ. Let everyone who is permitted by heavenly providence to enter the priesthood consider himself a servant and a slave to his brethren, as is said by the Lord of lords and head of Principalities, "For who is greater, he who sits at the table, or he who serves? Is it not he who sits at the table? Yet I am among you as the One who serves" (Luke 22:27).

May the Lord have mercy on His priests and congregation, and enlighten everyone's heart to know the meaning of service. How sublime is its honour, and how great is its reward. When a servant is called by God and not by people, may he be crowned with the crown of humility, for humility is a grace granted to complete all virtues and is also the basis for carrying on all virtues. We ask this through the intercessions of St Mary and all the saints. Amen.

26 July 1970

Hardened Hearts

"He has blinded their eyes and hardened their hearts, lest they should see with their eyes, lest they should understand with their hearts and turn, so that I should heal them" (John 12:40). This is the prophecy of Isaiah the Prophet, and although it is spoken about those who did not believe in the Lord Jesus Christ, it still applies today with the children of God and the believers. It is seen when the truth is very clear, yet the person in front of you does not want to be convinced, even if everyone else is trying to convince them. That is why, just before this verse, the Lord of Glory says, "walk while you have the light, lest darkness overtake you; he who walks in darkness does not know where he is going" (John 12:35). Here, we see the meaning of having our eyes blinded. May the Lord protect us from this and make us live, and walk in unity with His light, for He is the Light that shines on everyone in the world.

The Prophet also refers to the hardness of the heart of a person who is not living and following the truth, for the heart is the greatest guide to the way of life. We often hear how hard the saints work to plough the ground of their hearts in order to hear the voice of God, so He becomes their guide and light, lighting their way to the correct path leading to eternal life (John 6:45).

Blessed are the eyes that can recognise the correct path. Blessed are the pure hearts that feel the truth and God who is all in all, "But blessed are your eyes for they see, and your ears for they hear" (Matt 13:16).

17 August 1971

❦ ❦ ❦

"No one engaged in warfare entangles himself with the affairs of this life, that he may please him who enlisted him as a soldier. And also if anyone competes in athletics, he is not crowned unless he competes according to the rules" (2 Tim 2:4,5). Here, our great teacher St Paul teaches us the legacy of struggle, and the successful struggle is the one chosen and decided for us by the Lord. In verse four above, monks learn how our early fathers succeeded and won victory in their spiritual lives. How they gained sublime virtues, and how strong their relationship was with their Lord. They found favour in His eyes; He rejoiced in them and loved them till the end.

This is because they abandoned everything in this world with all its pleasures and desires and simply followed Him. They lived in caves, in the wilderness, and on mountains, not out of fear or because of failure in life, but so that they could empty their hearts and minds of all worldly things to prepare and consecrate them as a dwelling for the Lord. "For what profit is it to a man if he gains the whole world, and loses his own soul?" (Matt 16:26)

Our teacher St Paul the Apostle teaches us that a soldier equipped with the weapons of faith and prayer, who dedicates his time to prayer and is alert to face spiritual struggle is the one who wins and gains the crown. The one who neglects his spiritual canons and duties, and is careless in following the Lord's commandments and the teachings of the Desert Fathers, resembles a soldier who has thrown his weapons away and slept on the battlefield, giving the enemy a chance to conquer him. "Therefore take up the whole armor of God" (Eph 6:13) and "blessesd are those servants whom the master, when he comes, will find watching" (Luke 12:37).

May the Lord make us, His honest soldiers, deserving of His monastic call and ready for the Kingdom of Heaven through the intercessions of His Blessed Mother and all His saints. Amen.

24 October 1971

❧   ⬥   ☙

Hypocrisy

"And when all the people heard Him, even the tax collectors justified God, having been baptised with the baptism of John. But the Pharisees and lawyers rejected the will of God for themselves, not having been baptised by him" (Luke 7:29,30).

Here "all the people" refers to the general congregation. Usually they are the simple ones who quickly and accept the word of God. To everyone, the tax collectors were viewed as sinners, and the Lord Jesus was blamed for sitting and eating with them. The Pharisee justified himself by claiming that he was not like the tax collector.

Similarly in the spiritual life, the simple are aware of their weaknesses and have a good relationship with God. Particularly in monasticism, those who fill the caves and mountains are those who feel that they know and can do nothing, proving the Lord's words, "My strength is made perfect in weakness." (2 Cor 12:9).

The simple were victorious in their struggle against the enemy and able to conquer them by the blood of the Lamb. As for the Pharisees and those who blindly followed the Mosaic law, they rejected the Lord's words and depended on their own knowledge and abilities. They were the ones saying, "With our tongue we will prevail; our lips are our own" (Ps 12:4) They are the ones who cared about the cleanness of the cup and the whitewashing of the tomb from the outside, depending on their own knowledge and keeping Moses' law. They are the ones whom Jesus rebuked for their hard-hearted ways, saying, "Woe to you."

Let us remain aware, lest we only keep the commandments on the surface. Let us dig deeper and ensure that we are building on rock so that our building is strong and steadfast, avoiding potentially ruining that great house. As it says in the Scriptures "and the ruin of that house was great" (Luke 6:49).

May the Lord have mercy on us, and crown our struggle peacefully. We ask this through the intercession of the Mother of God and all the saints. Amen

18 December 1971

※》 ᴬ⳩(ᴄᴄ)ᴄᴷ ᴷᴷ

Having Faith

"For by faith you stand" (2 Cor 1:24).

A monk cannot bear the hardships of monastic life unless he is strong in his faith in the Lord Jesus Christ. Christ supports and helps him, just as He saved the three young men from the fiery furnace. He also saved Daniel from the lions' den; He preserved Joseph's chastity, and cured Job of all his calamities. A monk should also have faith in the monastic path, believing that this is his style of life to the end. He who repents cannot live a life of worry and doubt at the same time, "in returning and rest you shall be saved; in quietness and confidence shall be your strength." (Isaiah 30:15)… "The Lord is my portion, says my soul" (Lam 3:24). A monk should sincerely believe that all his toils for the love of God is not in vain, "Therefore the LORD will wait, that He may be… For the LORD is a God of justice; Blessed are all those who wait for Him" (Isaiah 30: 18). Also, as St Paul says: "But the Lord is faithful, who will establish you and guard you from the evil one" (2 Thess 3:3-4).

Life in the monastery strengthens faith, through steady prayers, repentance, and following the commandments. This is the life of a monk when he is ordained and the funeral prayer is prayed on him. A dead person does not desire a certain position in the world, nor inside the monastery.

He who really feels that he is dead considers himself last, thus he tolerates insults and humiliation. He never yearns to be the leader over his brethren, but only gives guidance if someone comes for a word of comfort or advice, "Bear one another's burdens, and so fulfill the law of Christ" (Gal 6:2). No power in the whole world can shake the life of such a monk who meets the Lord Jesus and intimately interacts with Him for years, awaiting the release of his soul from his body to be with his beloved, and from here (the monastery) he takes his crown.

4 February 1972

❧ ✦✦✦✦ ❧

Repentance

"Your sun shall no longer go down, nor shall your moon withdraw itself; for the Lord will be your everlasting light, and the days of your mourning shall be ended" (Isaiah 60:20).

"And the days of your mourning shall be ended" may mean the acceptance of your repentance. As monasticism is a life of repentance, a monk spends his life in prayer, worship, and humility until the grace of God shines within him and he feels the work of the Holy Spirit that comforts and calms him. Therefore he loses interest in worldly desires. Finally, his mind will be occupied with only heavenly matters. Purity of heart is the source of it all, for the heart becomes the dwelling place for God. These are the fruits of the Spirit, a sign of the monk's spiritual maturity is when he reaps the fruits after having worked hard planting and watering, "He who continually goes forth weeping, Bearing seed for sowing, shall doubtless come again with rejoicing, bringing his sheaves with him" (Ps 126:6).

15 March 1972

❧❧❧   ❧❦❧   ❦❦❦

The Wilderness

"I will even make a road in the wilderness and rivers in the desert. The beast of the field will honor Me, the jackals and the ostriches, because I give waters in the wilderness and rivers in the desert, to give drink to My people, My chosen. This people I have formed for Myself; they shall declare My praise" (Is 43:19-21).

Isn't this a prophecy about monasticism, and the worshippers in the mountains, wilderness and deserts? When he says, "rivers in the desert," this refers to the souls who deserted the world and came to the desert to be filled with the waters of grace and of the Holy Spirit, as our Lord says, "If anyone thirsts, let him come to Me and drink" (John 7:37). The words, "the beast of the field will honour Me, the jackals and the ostriches," is also a reflection of monasticism, which includes people with all sorts of different characters and habits. For example, St Moses the Black, who was a person with wild habits and fierce characteristics, repented and became a great saint. There is many other examples.

When monks live in the wilderness, practice repentance, and obtain humility, they become full of virtue and merits, like streams of spiritual teaching and deep experience. Out of the wilderness came many great teachers and leaders who blessed the entire world and preserved the faith. This is the meaning of the divinely inspired words, "My people, My chosen."

20 March 1972

Spiritual Growth

"Therefore, laying aside all malice, all deceit, hypocrisy, envy and all evil speaking" (1 Peter 2:1,2).

Herein lies the secret of the work of the Holy Spirit and His power in the saints. Being monks or elders who have spent many years in monasticism means nothing to the progress of our spiritual life unless we strive to plant these virtues within ourselves, "laying aside all malice, all deceit, hypocrisy, envy and all evil speaking." If these things do exist, then this is proof of being spiritual immature. We all know that an infant's food is milk; the mind is also nourished only by the pure grace of God, in which there is no evil at all, because "unless you are converted and become as little children, you will by no means enter the kingdom of heaven" (Matt 18:3).

This is the condition for growing and becoming united with God. From this point, we can easily discover how monks may deviate from the right path. We sometimes consider that practicing superficial fasting and prayer in monasticism is sufficient, and that we can keep rotten bones hidden in whitewashed tombs. We need to humble ourselves and sit at the feet of our Saviour, for He is the only one who can raise the dead with a single word, and lift us out of our sin and weakness. He is the one who can give us grace, power and spiritual growth if He sees our great yearning for His blessings, as it is said in the psalm: "May He grant you according to your heart's desire" (Ps 20:4). This is what the saints have struggled with daily, keeping their hearts pure, "Blessed are the pure in heart, for they shall see God" (Matt 5:8).

3 August 1972

Knowing your Calling

"But also for this very reason, giving all diligence, add to your faith virtue, to virtue knowledge, to knowledge self-control…

Therefore, brethren, be even more diligent to make your call and election sure, for if you do these things you will never stumble" (2 Peter 1:5,6,10).

How wonderful it is for a person to complete his call, steadfast to the end. Every calling has its struggle, but mixing two paths is wrong, St Isaac the Syrian said: "If you are a layman, live as one, and if you are a monk live as a solitary, but if you try to live both lives you will fail." Also St Peter the Apostle says, "Therefore, brethren, be even more diligent to make your call and election sure" (2 Peter 1:10). As the devil knows that you will gain fruits because of steadfastness, he will keep distracting your thoughts and trying to pull you out of the monastery to fulfill his destructive aim.

St Peter finishes the verse saying, "for if you do these things you will never stumble." Remaining steady and firm in your principles as a monk means you will obtain great protection against sin and failure, thus St Peter orders us to be "diligent." This is not an easy thing; it takes struggle, persistence and hard work. Therefore, do not live at ease and give your soul the chance to choose. The path of the Lord is a straightforward one; may the Lord make us steadfast in fulfilling our call.

9 August 1972

Divine Plan

"then hear in heaven Your dwelling place, and forgive, and act, and give to everyone according to all his ways, whose heart You know, for You alone know the hearts of all the sons of men" (1 Kings 8:39).

This was King Solomon's prayer at the consecration of the temple he built for the Lord. From the verse "give to everyone according to all his ways, whose heart You know," we clearly see that God looks at the heart. With all the good and bad things happening to people around us, we simply put our hands to our lips and repeat with David the Prophet, "I was mute, I did not open my mouth, because it was You Who did it" (Ps 39:9).

God tests the heart and knows what is hidden deep inside. He gives to each person according to his heart's wish, "May He grant you according to your heart's desire" (Ps 20:4). We also call Him 'the Almighty' as He knows our individual conditions and the desires of our hearts, whether good or bad, as well as our inner thoughts. We often wonder at certain situations that we see, which according to our human estimation are unacceptable, and yet we forget that everything is done with sublime wisdom and divine purpose. If we reflect back after the event, we find out that whatever happened was for the best. Let us give glory to our great God who gives everyone his heart's desire. Let us give our lives into His hands in faith, depending totally on Him, and submitting all our worries and sufferings to Him, for He wants only the best for us. Glory be to Him forever.

11 August 1972

The Narrow Gate

"Enter by the narrow gate; for wide is the gate and broad is the way that leads to destruction, and there are many who go in by it. Because narrow is the gate and difficult is the way which leads to life, and there are few who find it" (Matt 7:13,14).

This is the Lord's order and the constitution of the Christian life in general. Belief in the Lord Jesus Christ and our hope of enjoying eternal life mean it is essential to enter by the narrow gate. This gate means carrying the cross daily, as our Lord says that we will face tribulations in this world. We face tribulations because we are fulfilling His commandments. Thus, there is always a struggle between the will of goodness and the power of evil. The gate of desire, enjoyment, evil, hypocrisy, pride, deceit, etc. is wide; anyone can get through it. Few, though, will enter by the narrow gate, which leads to eternity, and they find it only through digging, searching and hardship, "the kingdom of heaven suffers violence, and the violent take it by force" (Matt 11:12).

If this is the case for the Christian laymen, what about the monks who have died to the world, with all its desires and ranks? Hence nowadays there are many calamities and there is much confusion on the correct monastic life, an ideal monk is regarded by people according to his achievement in service and honour in the church. People do not know that all of these things are just weeds. The true fruits of the Spirit that St Paul described are acquired via an austere life, as practiced in the wilderness, deserts and caves by our early fathers.

Monks who struggle to take off the old man to gain these fruits are viewed with dismay by others. People claim they are a failure, as if they are introducing a new form of monasticism by entering by the narrow gate! As monks we need to know that service is very easy, but monasticism is very hard. We honour the servants chosen by God for a certain service, but service for a monk that includes outside ambitions has no spiritual depth at all. True monasticism means reaching spiritual depths that a layman cannot reach; the same applies to a monk serving in the world. So from this point, we understand the philosophy of genuine monastic life in the wilderness and deserts, for its aim and its struggle is digging and searching for the narrow gate.

This is why our Lord Jesus Christ says that few will find Him. We notice that nowadays few are joining the monastic movement, and even fewer monks are searching for the narrow gate. May our Lord grant us perfection and steadfastness to reach the narrow gate, for without Him and His grace we can do nothing.

19 August 1972

Self Love

"For men will be lovers of themselves…traitors, headstrong, haughty, lovers of pleasure rather than lovers of God, having the form of godliness but denying its power" (2 Tim: 3:2;4-5).

What a harsh saying, especially if it is about those who have consecrated their lives for the Lord. I am so afraid that this is a description of me as a monk.

There are many kinds of self love, which are clear to the person himself and to those surrounding him. But sometimes a person may be deceived, and the only thing that helps us to avoid loving ourselves and to follow the Lord's commandment is humility, "If anyone desires to come after Me, let him deny himself, and take up his cross, and follow Me" (Matt 16:24) . A truly humble person is a person who loves God, denies himself, and rejects all desires, the greatest of which is seeking authority.

This is a very dangerous disease, as explained by our early fathers the saints. They related to us how they reached the height of spirituality when they conquered all weakness rooted within the human soul. Human judgment is usually different to God's, because people look at the eyes while the Lord looks at the heart.

When reading the lives of the saints we see their total self denial. This is not an easy thing to achieve, for to live as an earthly angel requires great humility, caring for nothing in this life except pleasing the Lord and following His commandments.

22 August 1972

⫸ ᜦ℧᠍ᜦ ⫷

Self Denial

"Assuredly, I say to you, unless you are converted and become as little children, you will by no means enter the kingdom of heaven. Therefore whoever humbles himself as this little child is the greatest in the kingdom of heaven" (Matt 18:3-4).

We are living in an age of competition where everyone is competing to become the first, the best, or the greatest. But where is the self denial recommended by our Lord?

The more a person humbles himself, the higher he is in virtue. When St Moses the Black asked St Zachariah, "Who is the monk?" the latter took off his monastic hood, which denotes honour in monasticism, and put it under his feet, saying "If a monk is not like this, he cannot become a monk."

Many great saints escaped honour by pretending they were fools or insane, so that they would not fall into vainglory. Now it is the opposite. A monk wants to be a teacher before becoming a disciple. Although everyone admires the idea of self denial and humility, when it comes into practice through tribulations we see the opposite.

We need to be watchful, to concentrate on the Lord's words, "unless you are converted and become as little children, you will by no means enter the kingdom of heaven." The Lord is the one who preserves children. May He grant us His Grace.

24 August 1972

True Wisdom

"Let no one deceive himself. If anyone among you seems to be wise in this age, let him become a fool that he may become wise. For the wisdom of this world is foolishness with God. For it is written, 'He catches the wise in their own craftiness'" (1 Cor 3:18-19).

We have received God's Spirit so that we might know the things given to us by God and to preach them, for we are being taught by the Holy Spirit. "These things we also speak, not in words which man's wisdom teaches but which the Holy Spirit teaches, comparing spiritual things with spiritual. But the natural man does not receive the things of the Spirit of God, for they are foolishness to him; nor can he know them, because they are spiritually discerned. But he who is spiritual judges all things, yet he himself is rightly judged by no one" (1 Cor 2:13-15).

How wonderful are these verses, in which St Paul the teacher and philosopher expresses the work of the Holy Spirit in the soul. He considers the wisdom of this world as foolishness when compared to the Spirit of God dwelling within His saints. Based on this spiritual measurement, the prophets of the Old Testament prophesied and the apostles in the New Testament preached salvation and spread its message throughout the entire world (Rom 10:18). Our saintly fathers lived in the wilderness and deserts with this same Spirit and the world did not deserve even their footsteps. Many philosophers and scientists approached them and sat at their feet to quench their thirst for spirituality through the heavenly wisdom given to them by the Lord of wisdom: "These things we also speak, not in words which man's wisdom teaches but which the Holy Spirit teaches." There is only One true teacher as our Lord says, "But the Helper, the Holy Spirit, whom the Father will send in My name, He will teach you all things, and bring to your remembrance all things that I said to you" (John 14:26).

So how can we acquire the work of the Holy Spirit within ourselves in this spiritually feeble era, when the world is prevailing with all its desires and lust? The only remedy is to go back and meditate deeply and seriously on the lives of our early fathers, the saints, who found favour with their God. He poured His grace on them as they sought Him with all their hearts, expelling all of the idols of lust from their hearts. The Lord is honest in His promises. He gives generously and freely to the ones who seek Him earnestly and those who never look back as Lot's wife did. There in the silence and serenity of the wilderness, where the monks renounce all worldly desires and are united with their Creator, the grace of God works within hundreds and thousands of humble monks. They empty their hearts from all vanity, so they are ready to be filled by the Lord.

3 March 1973

※ ※ ※

The Way of the Fathers

"...but imitate those who through faith and patience inherit the promises" (Heb 6:12).

Everyone is searching and looking for ways to reach God; one person prefers fasting and asceticism, another prefers staying up all night and being poor by choice, another chooses chastity, while another is very active in his service, and so on.

While I am the least of them, I say in my simplicity that there is nothing better than clinging to the Lord. Mary, who was praised by the Lord, simply sat at His Feet, listening to His words and looking at His face, in order to be united with Him. Her silence and meditation is the greatest proof of her love for the Lord Jesus Christ, glory be to Him.

The sinful woman who bathed His feet with perfume was forgiven all her sins because she loved Him so much. This act of love is also a result of clinging to the Lord. When I say clinging to the Lord, I do not mean we should neglect the struggle to acquire different virtues, but we cannot concentrate totally on them, as if they are the aim in our spiritual life. They are simply a means of helping us to draw closer and closer to abiding in the love of the Lord. When He sees our patience in knocking at His door, He will never let us down. He may take time to test our faith in His love, then when He is sure of our faithfulness and honesty, He will pour the streams of His great love on us.

We are only dust, yet out of His love for us, God purifies us with His grace and dwells within us, filling our hearts with His love and our tongues with His praise. Thus, all our deeds will be from Him and through Him, "for without Me you can do nothing" (John 15:5).

How can we gain the Lord if we are not clinging to Him, waiting for His work in us? This is our hope as it was the hope of our early Desert Fathers, who lived in caves in the wilderness and in monasteries.

May their blessings be with us all. Amen.

6 April 1973

⋙ ⁘⧼☯⧽⁘ ⋘

Being Led by the Spirit

'For as many as are led by the Spirit of God, these are sons of God" (Rom 8:14).

This is the trademark of a successful person; checking ourselves before condemning others. Am I a person led by the Spirit of God? Do I give the grace of God a chance to work in me and through me so that I can see His great deeds in my weak self? Do I follow St Mary's example of keeping everything in her heart? Do I depend on my personal experiences and education and plan for every occasion?

Here, the cunning devil interferes with all my deeds to distract me from following the Lord Christ and from His grace within me. Finally, I discover the bitter fact; all the things I have achieved have collapsed because they were built on sand, depending on myself. I did not yield to the grace of God, nor seek guidance from the pious men of God in humility. This is seen very clearly in the life of worship and monasticism. We have never heard, and will never hear, of any monk who made spiritual progress or acquired any grace as a result of his human power. We are not ignoring the various struggles and wars in the monastic path, however they are useless if they are not supported by the grace of God. It is exactly like the work of fire in coal, or the need for leaves to preserve the fruit of the trees.

Nothing is more beautiful and joyful for a monk than to wait for the work of grace of God within him, no matter how long it takes. All of the fights, struggles, and wars with the devils that a monk faces are part of the life of submission. He has given his life as a sacrifice of love to the Lord Jesus Christ. Thus, he is truly led by the Spirit of God, and deserves to be called a son of God. How great is this sonship and honourable title to the poor humble monk, who becomes one of God's special sons, ready to inherit the Kingdom, "For as many as are led by the Spirit of God, these are sons of God."

16 July 1973

"Then Jesus said to them, "Do not be afraid. Go and tell My brethren to go to Galilee, and there they will see Me." (Matt 28: 10)

"Then the eleven disciples went away into Galilee, to the mountain which Jesus had appointed for them…but some doubted." (Matt 28: 16-17)

This is the commandment of the Lord, that whoever seeks to see Him, he must go to Galilee, where He is visibly seen. On the mountain, the fog of worries and various sins will be lifted from our hearts. The monastic fathers teach us how to purify our hearts, as they obtained the purity of heart on mountains and in lives spent in deserts; lives of quietness and tranquility in monastires, where they experienced the verse "Blessed are the pure in heart, for they shall see God". The disciples went to the mountain where the Lord ordered them to go, "When they saw Him, they worshiped Him; but some doubted." These words have strong connotations, and they show its powerful effect over the years and centuries until this day. Those who worship God, they worship Him in Spirit and truth, but whoever doubts will never reach his goal, and his love will never be complete. Many have come to this life of monasticism, and when time passed, and they could not see Christ, and they kept waiting to see the revelation, and when they still could not see it, they went back. It was the cloud of temptation and various other struggles, which was supposed to accompany them to see Christ, has made them doubt in the reliability of the revelation; they did not know that 'with your patience you will possess your soul.'

However, those who worshiped Jesus, did so out of submission to His will, and in want of fulfilling His commandment, and bearing everything set in their path. Whether they see the revelation or not, or whether their eyes are capable of seeing or they have been dirtied, their concern is still to fulfil the commandments of the Lord, "...to go to Galilee, and there they will see Me."

This is our faith in our Lord Jesus Christ, that He is honest and just in fulfilling His promises. Whoever looks upon Him, his face will shine and be enlightened, and will not be ashamed. Steadfastness in the calling of the Lord is evident for us, and this in itself is a revelation coming out of a strong faith in Christ. However hard it may be to go up the mountain, it will inevitably bring a monk who rejoices in the calling of the Lord, to receive a pure heart, and thus be able to see Him.

However, whoever doubts, and goes back, then the enemy will receive him and drown him in the waves of this world. He will not know where he is going because darkness has covered his eyes, and fear has defeated him. For this reason, the Lord says to His children, "Do not fear."

Truly, when they saw Him, they worshipped Him, but some doubted. May the Lord make us worthy to be true worshippers in Spirit and truth, hating the lusts of the world and its glory, and my soul shall chant 'The LORD is my portion, therefore I hope in Him!

10 February 1974

"And my speech and my preaching were not with persuasive words of human wisdom, but in demonstration of the Spirit and of power, that your faith should not be in the wisdom of men but in the power of God." (1 Cor 2: 4-5)

We know that the power of the Christian faith is not in the influence of words or earthly wisdom, but through the power of the Holy Spirit, and His work in the non-believer. For this reason, it was very difficult to preach to pagan worshippers, and non Christians. True and successful service is not words in sermons, as much as it is the work of the Holy Spirit in the servant and in the listener. For the Spirit must go forth and prepare the ears to listen to accept the word of God.

29 April 1974

www.ingramcontent.com/pod-product-compliance
Lightning Source LLC
Chambersburg PA
CBHW022123080426
42734CB00006B/229